Barbara C. Vasiloff

Teaching Self-Discipline to Children

15 Essential Skills

TWENTY-THIRD PUBLICATIONS

185 WILLOW STREET • PO BOX 180 • MYSTIC, CT 06355
TEL: 1-800-321-0411 • FAX: 1-800-572-0788
E-MAIL: ttpubs@aol.com • www.twentythirdpublications.com

Teaching Self-Discipline to Children

15 Essential Skills

Twenty-Third Publications
A Division of Bayard
185 Willow Street
P.O. Box 180
Mystic, CT 06355
(860) 536-2611 or (800) 321-0411
www.twentythirdpublications.com
ISBN:1-58595-272-9

Library of Congress Catalog Card Number: 2003104397
Printed in the U.S.A.

Dedication

To my mother and father
Ann and George Vasiloff
for showing me how to live a faith-filled disciplined life.

Acknowledgements

The late Msgr. John Flynn for continued encouragement in developing the Discipline with Purpose program; Paula Lenz, for original program development and continued support and belief that children can be taught self-discipline; Diane Flynn and Liz Kearney, educators and DWP consultants who help to broaden skill concepts; Patti Bailey, for the guided meditations; Kathy Paape, Dan McShane, and the San Xavier Indian Mission, Tucson, AZ, for the illustrations of the fifteen skills; Christine Przybocki Ryktarsyk, for the original poetry and illustrations; Jo Mersnick, for the music that accompanies several skills; Caroline O' Connell and Denise Dufek, for the children's literature recommendations; and the countless teachers who used and developed lessons to go with the fifteen skills.

Contents

Introduction

What should a catechist or Catholic educator know about discipline and self-discipline?

It's no accident that the words "disciple" and "discipline" are spelled so much alike. Both come from two Latin root words, *discipulus*, which means a disciple, and *discere*, which means to learn. Both "disciple" and "discipline" have a place in catechesis.

There are three occasions when an adult can feel comfortable disciplining others:

- whenever someone is in physical or psychological danger;
- whenever someone is being abusive in tone or gesture;
- whenever someone is out of control or has pushed beyond the limits of reasonable action.

In these circumstances immediate swift action with a resulting consequence is warranted. Most of the behaviors children engage in do not fall into this category. Most of children's annoying or unwanted behaviors demonstrate a lack of self-discipline or self-direction. Their behaviors indicate that they have not yet acquired the skills or developmental maturity to choose to act appropriately.

To become self-disciplined a person must acquire information about how he or she uniquely acts in life. This information is primarily gained through reflection on Scripture, life experience, and the guidance of others in pointing out the skills we do well or poorly. When catechists understand the skills that lead a person to become self-disciplined:

- they have a framework that will provide direction and purpose to a child who is in the process of growing up;
- they are able to distinguish between behaviors that call for disciplinary actions and behaviors that need to be taught;
- they can help children practice gospel actions in daily life;
- children can become conscious of the choices they make that help or hinder a community;

- children and adults can be challenged to use their skills to change conditions that are unjust or harmful to others;
- the catechist can model self-discipline skills while interacting with others.

What is self-discipline?

Self-discipline is a person's ability to wait. While you wait you think and process and decide how to act. Waiting is the master skill that helps people delay impulsive behavior. Character, virtue, the corporal and spiritual works of mercy, the beatitudes are all the result of self-discipline.

How does a person become self-disciplined? Author Thomas Power writes,

Before a child is developmentally age five the ability to self-regulate and his internal motivation to choose to do the right thing (AKA conscience) are not fully developed and present in the absence of an adult.

Children can be taught the foundation of self-discipline from birth until they are developmentally five years of age. This foundation can be summarized in this way. Children need to be taught in the most loving way that there is a will stronger than their own, and that they are not the center of the universe. This is best accomplished by adults who know and understand how the child grows and develops; are consistent in their actions; model appropriate interactive behaviors; are willing to be available to meet the basic needs of the child; and are not afraid to discipline when a child's action is dangerous, abusive, or harmful.

Catechists can help children learn that they cannot have all of their needs met at the expense of others. Caring teachers use the fear of punishment (consequences), the promise of a reward, and the child's desire to please as strong external motivators to discipline children. At the same time they can begin the process of teaching self-discipline skills to their students.

What are the fifteen self-discipline skills?

Fifteen natural opportunities for people to practice waiting are present in daily life. These opportunities are so natural that often they are missed or taken for granted. In 1984, while teaching religious education, Paula Lenz and I identified fifteen skills that give people an opportunity to practice this kind of self-disciplined waiting. These skills are as follows:

1. Listening

2. Following instructions

3. Asking questions

4. Sharing time, space, people, and things

5. Using social skills

6. Working cooperatively

7. Understanding and explaining reasons for rules

8. Accomplishing tasks on your own

9. Demonstrating leadership

10. Communicating effectively

11. Organizing time, space, people, and things

12. Resolving problems

13. Initiating solutions

14. Distinguishing fact from feeling

15. Making sacrifices and/or serving others.

The fifteen skill framework is used to measure growth in self-directed behavior.

In this book, the self-discipline skills are grouped into three categories. While children of all ages can be taught something about all fifteen skills, there are certain ages when the skills will be difficult for children to demonstrate on their own without an external cue or coaching from an adult.

The first five skills are called basic skills and are necessary for interacting with others. These are difficult for children in kindergarten through the end of grade three to master.

Around the age of nine or ten, children can learn another important lesson: how to live in a democratic environment. The second five self-discipline skills are called the constructive skills. Children in grades four through seven are developmentally ready to learn these five skills.

Five additional skills are learned from grades eight through high school. These last five skills are called generative skills and require a more comprehensive worldview. People are motivated to demonstrate these higher level skills when the needs of others can be recognized and are considered important.

Why do we talk about self-discipline as skills?

Three adults I know recently set a goal of learning how to use a computer. Tonya looked at the manuals that came with the software and quickly threw them into a box. She picked up the phone and called her friend who was computer literate. She asked him to show her how to run the computer. Step by step, with the help of a buddy, Tonya mastered this introductory computer phase.

When Denise picked up the computer manuals she sat down with a yellow highlighter. Reading through the introductory chapter she highlighted the steps she wanted to remember. This took her several hours. During this time, she never touched the computer. Only after she had internalized what she wanted to do on the computer did she boot it up. Once Denise was ready internally, she was willing to show the world what she could do with this skill.

Bernie put the monitor, keyboard, and hard drive together by looking at the pictures, plugs, and cords. Through trial and error he began to use the machine. He turned it on, started punching keys, and used the mouse to investigate what the machine could do. Before the week was over Bernie had taken most of the machine apart and put it back together. This hands-on approach would continue indefinitely until he reached the state of perfection he wanted—or until he became discouraged.

Today, Tonya, Denise, and Bernie are all computer literate. All have

Skills are not the same as rules. When rules are established and then not followed, consequences occur. You can't break a skill! When a skill is missing or not yet mastered, the person is given another chance to practice the skill. An adult usually provides additional information or coaching to help the student succeed. It has been said that it takes between seventeen and twenty-one practices before someone learning a new skill feels comfortable performing that skill.

SELF-DISCIPLINE IS THE ABILITY TO WAIT AND THINK

1. When we listen we *wait* to speak. We *think*: Do I understand what the speaker is saying? Do I have a question? Can I do what is suggested?

2. When we follow instructions we *wait* for the speaker to finish giving directions. We *think*: Can I repeat the steps in my plan of action?

3. When we ask questions we *wait* for a speaker to finish speaking. We *think*: Am I curious about anything the speaker has said? What words will I use to ask my question? Do I know the criteria for a good question?

4. When we share time we *wait* our turn. We *think*: How will I use the time when it is my turn? When we share space we *wait* until others have moved out of the space we plan to move into. We *think*: How high can I count before it is my turn to get into that space?
When we share people we *wait* until the person is available to get their attention. We *think*: Is there anything I can do to help myself?
When we share things we *wait* for others to finish using materials. We *think*: What condition will the object be in when I get it? How can I make sure I return it in the same or better condition?

5. When we use social skills we *wait* until we have noticed another person. We *think*: How can I make this person feel comfortable and at ease?

6. When we cooperate we *wait* for everyone to finish their task. We *think*: Can I help anyone else? Is my part the best it can be? Can I make improvements?

7. When we understand the reasons for rules we *wait* and learn if rules have already been made. We *think*: Do I know the reason for this rule? Who can I ask if I do not understand why the rule has been made? What process is needed to get the rule changed?

8. When we learn on our own how to accomplish a task we *wait* until we have learned the boundaries or rules for finishing the task. We *think*: Do I know how to do the job? What plan of action will get this job done? Can I do the entire job or just a portion of it?

9. When we are a leader we *wait* until we have noticed a situation that needs a leader. We *think*: What course of action will make life better for people? Are the needs of another important to me? Am I willing to act even if I am the only one? Am I willing to be inconvenienced for the sake of another?

10. When we communicate we *wait* until the other person finishes speaking. We *think*: What words can I use that will correctly represent what I want to say?

11. When we organize time, space, people, or things we *wait* until we get a mental image of the way things are to be ordered. We *think*: What design, time-frame, schedule, containers, or space will work the best?

12. When we resolve problems of mutual concern we *wait* until we can understand the problem from more than one point of view. We *think*: How can I state the problem from two different points of view? What solution will make us both winners?

13. When we take the initiative to solve a problem we *wait* until we notice that a problem exists. We *think*: How can I name the problem so others will understand it? What solution will make all parties winners?

14. When we separate fact from feeling we *wait* until we have neutralized strong emotions. We *think*: What name can I put on my feelings? Where do I experience these feelings in my body? What are the things I can do nothing about? What can I change?

15. When we serve others and make sacrifices we *wait* to have our needs or desires met while we put other's needs and desires first. We *think*: What am I willing to let go of or give up so life will be better for others?

acquired a new skill. All three knew the goal they wanted to reach and had the freedom to reach it using their particular learning style and motivational method.

It's the same with self-discipline skills. People acquire these through practice, using their own unique learning style. For example, when learning the skill of following instructions, people might use one of the following three methods.

1. Some people learn to follow instructions when they are given a list of the steps involved to read and think about. They privately practice the steps, and when they feel internally ready they are able to demonstrate how the instructions were followed.

2. Some people need a buddy or partner to show them how to do the skill. They ask questions as they go and check to make sure they are doing things correctly. Once shown a skill, they imitate the steps and make the skill their own.

3. Some people use the trial and error method. They begin work before all the instructions are even given. Through coaching and correction, they adjust until they complete the instructions. But they can also lose interest and settle for a less than completed project if correction is too harsh or too constant. With humor and a person they trust, they will accept correction and continue to practice the skill.

How does it work?

The fifteen self-discipline skills provide adults and children with a common way to talk about growing up and becoming self-directed. As a religious educator, I have found that the skills provide students with daily examples of how they can live out gospel values. The self-discipline framework challenges them to set personal goals and push beyond their comfort level in learning to work with others.

Opportunities to practice these fifteen skills extend far beyond the religion classroom. Children and teens soon become aware of times and places when the situation calls for demonstrating one or more of the self-discipline skills. They notice that being self-disciplined can help people work together and build strong relationships—just as the inability to be self-disciplined can cause tension in relationships and build walls between people.

Children of all ages can perform all fifteen self-discipline skills discussed in this book if they are helped to do so. Each person will find that some skills are easier to master than others. The child with a learning difficulty may struggle with the skills of listening and following instructions, for example. He or she may, however, be excellent at demonstrating sharing and sacrificing. Gifted students who are good communicators often struggle with the skill of cooperation. They find it difficult to work with others when they are competent to complete work independently.

The same is true for adults. As a catechist you may be a terrific organizer and have well-developed lessons prepared each week. But if you are not also a person who can listen and separate fact from feeling, your children may not become engaged in the activities you have planned. Likewise, if you are an excellent listener but lack the ability to organize a block of time to accomplish a task, little productive work might be done in your classroom.

Practicing and learning self-discipline skills is necessary for both children and adults. Thinking about appropriate behavior keeps our attitude and language neutral. We avoid the risk of passing blame or criticizing personalities when we discuss behaviors in skill language.

How do I teach self-discipline, or the skills of waiting?

Learning the skills of self-discipline is a lifelong process. As we grow and mature, our ability to practice self-discipline changes—hopefully to keep pace with our lives. Here follow some guidelines to help you teach self-discipline to your students:

1. *Learn these facts about self-discipline:*

- Self-discipline is a person's ability to wait. While waiting a person thinks and decides how to act.

- Fifteen natural opportunities to practice waiting already exist in daily life.

- Since skills are observable, other people can tell if a person is self-disciplined or not. When a person cannot or chooses not to practice a skill it remains hidden or locked inside the person.

- Each person must choose to use their skills.

- Skills can be called inner powers or hidden skills. The word "power" comes from two Greek words which mean "the *ability* to do something" and "the *capacity* to do something." In regard to self-discipline skills, power implies that a person knows about the fifteen skills and chooses to use them as needed.

2. *Introduce students to the skills by using illustrations.* This book contains illustrations that have been developed by catechists and teachers in primary, intermediate, and junior high settings to help children internalize the self-discipline skills. These illustrations are found on the guided meditation page for each chapter.

- The first five skills, referred to as basic skills, use drawings that students in preschool through fourth grade may find helpful in forming an image of how a person might act when they perform that skill.

- Skill six through ten, the constructive skills, contain drawings developed by a Native American artist in Tucson, Arizona. These illustrations help students in grades four to six begin to understand how these skills are valued in different cultures.

- Skills eleven through fifteen, the generative skills, use drawings by Dan McShane, a high school senior. In each of these illustrations Dan included his own text to highlight how students in grades seven through ten might think about these skills. The figures in these drawings have blank faces so each student cn picture himself or herself in the illustration.

You can copy and enlarge these illustrations and give them to the children or teens. They can then use these pictures to create a reflection booklet or journal for their ideas, thoughts, images, and reactions. Each time a new skill is discussed, students can take notes about the skill and also record practices they will use to master the skill. The guided meditations encourage students to draw the images they shape from the meditation.

At the beginning of each chapter you will find another illustration that relates to a Scripture passage. These too can be copied and used by you or the students to reinforce the scriptural connection for each self-discipline skill.

3. *Decide to set aside five minutes each class time to do one or more of the following*:

- Allow time for youngsters to personally determine which skill they want to practice during the week. Provide time for them to record their goal and direct them to keep track of the practices.

- Invite children to report on times and places outside the religion class when they practiced a skill.

- Lead students in the scriptural meditation found with each skill. Allow time for them to illustrate or write about their meditation.

- Select one or more of the skill practices and invite students to learn about the skill and practice the skill.

- Teach youngsters the poetry or songs that accompany many of the skills.

- Read children a recommended children's literature book that highlights a skill.

- Use the teachable moment. As situations arise, give youngsters information about the skills.

4. *Many of the skills can be used within any gathering or class.* The skills do not have to be taught in order. However, when catechists first begin working with a group, many have found it helpful to discuss and practice these skills first: skill #1 (listening); skill #2 (following instructions); skill #7 (understanding the reason for rules); and skill #12 (problem solving). These four skills help set the structure for your time with the children and give guidelines for establishing effective classroom management.

5. *Take time to read and savor the contents of this book.* Focus on one skill at a time. Consider the reflection question shown at the beginning of each chapter. These questions can serve as a guide for helping your students engage in the many skill practices outlined in this book.Read the stories found throughout the book that highlight how a particular skill or skill language can be used. Become aware of when and how certain skills are needed in our lives. Reflect, too, on how often Jesus called on people in Scripture to demonstrate these skills.

6. *Share the list of fifteen self-discipline skills with parents.* Once the skill framework is introduced to youngsters, adults can use the framework as an objective standard for talking with children and parents about behavior, growing up, and living the gospel in daily life.

Jesus Models How We Are to Live and Teach Others

1. **Be open to change.** Jesus called his disciples to conversion, a change of heart. He called them to change, not just for the sake of change but to change for the sake of others. How willing are we to change, to grow in developing our own self-discipline skills? What skills of self-discipline have we mastered as educators? How do we consciously teach our children to master them?

2. **Act out of a belief system.** Jesus equipped his disciples with beliefs they could use as a framework for understanding the actions he asked of them. He reinforced their understanding of God as Father and asked them to think about the relationship between God and humans. What would this pattern mean in the life of an educator who wants to examine his or her beliefs in terms of how children learn to be self-disciplined?

3. **Have a positive outlook.** Jesus instructed his disciples that their attitude must be positive. They were chosen to serve, not to be served. When a person is called to service, they enter into a very positive way of looking at life. They bring happiness to others. As catechists and teachers, do we bring a positive attitude to our classroom? To our children? To our subject matter?

4. **Develop habits that lead to action.** Jesus encouraged his disciples to develop certain habits or ways of acting that would benefit others. He told them to pray unceasingly. He taught them that good habits meant feeding the hungry, clothing the naked, visiting the sick, counseling the ignorant. What are the habits or skills we must teach our children if they are to be self-disciplined? Here we must remember that we will be successful in teaching these skills to the degree that we possess them or are trying to master them in our own lives.

5. **Respect freedom.** Jesus always respected the free will of each person. Even when he raised questions that made his listeners think again about their actions or demanded that they do some searching or perhaps change, they were still left with the personal freedom to choose. How do we leave our children after a confrontation or encounter with us?

Summary

- When the fifteen skill framework is used by children and adults, it provides a common language and direction for growing up.
- Skills are observable so people can know if progress is being made in becoming self-disciplined.
- We can be patient with ourselves and children learning how to do a self-discipline skill, knowing that one of three methods will be used to acquire new skills.
- Demonstrating self-discipline and not giving in to impulsive behaviors is a way to live the gospel in our daily lives.

Reflection Questions

1. Why is it important for a catechist to understand the difference between discipline and self-discipline?

2. What do you think of the concept that self-discipline means a person's ability to "wait"?

3. What benefit do you see in having an objective standard to describe what it means for a person to be self-disciplined?

4. Which of the three methods described on page 4 do you use when you learn a new skill?

5. How does the fact that skills are not rules make a difference in your teaching—or not?

CHAPTER 1

Listening

Mary said, "Here am I, the servant of the Lord;
let it be with me according to your word." (Luke 1:38)

Reflection: How can I help my students listen to and hear God's word, as Mary did?

The six steps of listening are

1. Stop what I am doing or saying.
2. Clear away all distractions.
3. Look at or toward the person speaking.
4. Be able to tell the person what I heard.
5. Ask questions about what was not understood.
6. Do the task the speaker has requested.

A good listener

- Looks at the speaker.
- Is silent while someone speaks.
- Keeps his or her hands quiet.
- Doesn't look around the room.
- Doesn't talk while someone else is talking.
- Doesn't play with distracting objects.

GUIDED REFLECTION

LISTENING

As we begin our reflection, let's prepare to listen to a story from Scripture. Close your eyes. Take a quiet, deep breath and feel your body relax. Feel your feet and legs relax. Notice your arms and head feeling heavy. Your breathing has slowed down.

We are going to journey back in time. Let's go back 2,000 years. The world is a quiet place with no televisions, phones, computers, or cars to distract us. Picture a young girl named Mary. Mary lives in a small town called Nazareth. One day while Mary is alone in a small room, a bright light appears in the room. An angel moves out of the light toward her. The angel starts to speak to Mary. Look at Mary's face. What do you see?

The angel tells Mary that she is going to be the mother of God's Son. How does Mary look now? What does she do? Mary is confused by what she has heard and she asks the angel, "How can this be? I am not married." The angel replies, "With God, all things are possible. Do not worry how this will happen. Continue to trust God." Mary replies, "Behold, I am the handmaid of the Lord. May it be done to me according to your word." When the angel is gone, Mary sets out at once to visit her cousin Elizabeth. Mary wants to tell Elizabeth all that has happened to her

Picture Mary in your mind as God talks to her through the angel. What does she do? What does she look like as she listens to the news? Keep this image in your mind as you slowly open your eyes. Now take out your reflection booklet and draw a picture of anything you saw or heard during this reflection.

When most of the children have completed their illustrations, invite them to look at their pictures and describe what they saw or heard.

Engage in Discussion

Mary listened to the angel in this reflection. Look at each of the six steps of listening and tell a time when Mary used each of the steps.

Step 1: She stopped what she was doing.
Step 2: She cleared her distractions.
Step 3: She focused on the angel.
Step 4: She repeated what she heard to her cousin Elizabeth.
Step 5: She asked the angel, "But how can this be since I am not married?"
Step 6: She did what she was asked to do by saying, "May it be done to me according to your word."

Action Step

Each time someone asks you to listen today, think of Mary. She will be our model listener.

Tips for Teaching this Skill

Listening is the most basic skill and the foundation for all the rest. If children are unable or unwilling to do the first three steps of this skill, they are not ready to practice self-discipline. They are in need of discipline from the loving guidance of an external source.

- It is the only skill taught by having the children memorize six factual steps. All the other skills are learned by practicing exercises in which the skill is demonstrated.

- When children practice these six steps they are using a skill called focused listening. When we invite them to listen in this way, we should tell them how long they will be expected to stay in the listening position. The rule of thumb for someone to demonstrate focused listening is one minute per age of the listener.

- Teach the six steps of listening found on the opening page of this chapter along with the picture cues from page 13. Ask students to use their listening skill by using this prompt: "Please show me your listening skill."

- Teach this rhyme to children six or younger:

  If my eyes you cannot see,
  Don't begin to talk to me.

Make posters and small postcards with this rhyme. Place them around the classroom or in your home to remind everyone to wait until they can see the eyes or face of the person with whom they wish to communicate before speaking.

Skill Vocabulary

Use these phrases in class throughout the year to help reinforce the skill of listening:

- Please show me your listening skills.

- I'm distracted now and can't give you my full attention, do you still want to talk to me or wait until later?

- Please use your focused listening for _____ minutes.

- Tell me what you just heard me say.

- When you choose to listen there will be a benefit for you and everyone else around you.

How It Works

Marti was a first-year teacher who started teaching third graders several months ago. She was not comfortable in her role as a disciplinarian and hoped she would have children who could show some self-control. The first five days of school went remarkably well. At the start of the second week, she noticed that the children were taking longer and longer to come to attention when she asked them to do so. Side conversations were starting to break out, and the children talked even when she was trying to give instructions.

Marti consulted the list of the self-discipline skills and realized she had not talked with her class about any of the skills, especially the first one. She had assumed her children would know how to behave in class and believed her main job was to show them that she was a teacher who cared about them and the teaching profession.

The next day, Marti asked her twenty-eight third graders, "Who knows what I expect you to do when I ask you to listen?" A few children ventured to name the steps of listening: "We should open our ears and close our mouths. We should make sure our ears are clean so we can hear you. We should follow your instructions."

Marti took fifteen minutes to show and tell the youngsters what she would be looking for if they were using their self-discipline skill of listening. She told them there were three things they would have to do to get ready to listen:

1. Stop moving and talking.

2. Clear away distractions. (This usually means putting away everything you have in your hands.)

3. Look at or toward the person speaking.

She also told them that she knew people who could do these three steps and still not be listening. She introduced them to three more steps to use so that the speaker knew they actually heard what was being said.

4. Ask questions about what the speaker said.

5. Be able to say in your own words what you think you heard.

6. If you hear a direction given, as soon as the speaker is finished, begin to do what you heard.

Marti used masking tape to mark an X in the front and center of the classroom, showing students that whenever someone was standing on the X it was their cue to take their listening position. Each child made a postcard listing the six steps to keep as a reminder on their desk. Finally, each time she wanted them to use their self-discipline skill she would begin by saying, "Please show me your listening skill."

Not all of Marti's students have shown the ability to do this skill on their own without help. One or two of them have needed a partner or buddy to remind them when it is time to listen. But all of Marti's children know that when it is time to listen they are expected to be quiet and focus.

Activities

Magnetic Picture Cues

The picture cues found on page 13 illustrate the six steps of listening and can be used in many ways to make learning games. Here are two examples:

Enlarge and cut out the pictures. Laminate them and place a magnet on the back of each picture. Let young children put the six steps in order and place them on their refrigerator at home. Select one step each day to highlight or practice.

Matching Game

Mount each of the six picture cues from page 13 on a different color construction paper. Print the meaning of each cue on a separate piece of white paper. On the back of the written cues tape a small circle that is the same color as its corresponding illustrated cue.

Invite the children to match the words with the picture cues. When they think they have matched them correctly, they can turn over the word cues. If the colored circle matches the color of construction paper on which the illustrated cue is mounted, they will know they are correct. If not, they can practice learning the meaning of each cue again.

Listening Puzzle

Enlarge the picture found on page 13 and mount it on construction paper. Laminate the paper. Cut out the individual squares, mix them up, and invite students to put the puzzle back together.

Game of Chance

Start with a small white paper gift box in the shape of a cube (you can also get one from a paper supply store). Draw or copy one of the six steps of listening on each side of the cube. Enlarge the game board pictured on page 14. Mount it on construction paper. Obtain small tokens and a die to be used in the game. Let the first person toss the cube. If it lands on the stop sign—the first step of listening—the player can place their token on the board. They are then given another turn. If it does not land on the stop sign, the game continues to the next person. Continue in this fashion until a player has correctly identified all six steps of listening and has moved their token to each of the six spaces.

Decode the Message

Intermediate grade children can be challenged to discover the six steps of listening by practicing a higher level skill. As a team, they can work to figure out how to complete a worksheet. They will practice cooperation by figuring out on their own how to accomplish tasks.

Duplicate the handout on page 14. Make enough copies for each student. Divide the class into teams of four to do the exercise. Give the following instructions.

1. When I finish talking I will give each member of a team one sheet of paper.

2. Read the directions at the top and figure out on your own what you are supposed to do.

3. You will have ten minutes to work on this task.

Invite the children to ask questions on the topic before distributing the handout. They might ask:

- Why are we doing this? Response: "So all those who want to practice a self-discipline skill they will need as a grown-up will have an opportunity to do so."

- Do we have to do it? Response: "No, you must choose to practice the skill. If you choose not to, please find something to read or do while the rest of us work."

- Are we going to be graded? Response: "You will be asked to evaluate yourself by rating your practice of the skill on a scale from 1 to 5."

Listening Certificates

Engage children in grades three to nine in a discussion using these questions.

- Name a person you consider to be a good listener.
- What does that person/those persons do that impresses you?
- What two things can people do if they want to improve their listening habits?

At the end of the discussion complete the listening certificate found on page 15. Duplicate extra copies as needed for the children to give to their favorite listener(s).

Different Ways to Listen Appointment Card

Teach middle grade and junior high students the many different forms of listening. Duplicate the listening card found on page 15. Run off copies and place them in a strategic spot for all to use. Explain that they can tell others about the six different ways people can listen. Encourage them to use the cards whenever someone is in need of a good listener.

Listening and Doing

Invite youngsters to draw four geometric shapes: a square, circle, triangle, and rectangle. (Older students might want to add a trapezoid and a parallelogram.) Create statements that can be read to the students. A wide range of content areas can be included in this activity. Use this formula for the statements: If _____ then do this, but if _____ then do this. Here are some examples:

1. If today is Tuesday, then write your first name in the triangle; if today is not Tuesday print your first name inside the circle.

2. If Thomas was the apostle who betrayed Jesus, write the word Jesus in the circle; if another apostle was the one who betrayed Jesus, write that person's name in the square.

3. If we celebrate the coming of the Holy Spirit on Easter, draw a dove in the square; if we celebrate the coming of the Holy Spirit on Pentecost, draw a flower in the circle.

4. If Jesus died on a cross on the top of Mount Sinai, draw a cross in the triangle; if Jesus died on the cross on Mount Calvary, draw a cross in the square.

As children learn the formula they can be challenged to develop their own exercises to be given as a review or test to classmates.

Listening for Negatives

Enlarge and duplicate the puzzle found on page 16 Cut the pieces and place them in an envelope. Then invite students to:

1. Put the puzzle together.
2. Read the picture clues.
3. Solve the riddle.

Discuss with students:

- the answer to the riddle (the sun);
- clues that were helpful in solving the riddle;
- what all the puzzle clues have in common (use of the word "not").

Summarize by telling youngsters that this exercise gave them a chance to practice listening for negatives, words that tell what something is not. If a person can figure out what a thing is not, then it is easier to discover what it is.

Invite children to create another set of descriptions in which people will have to listen for negatives. Example: I am not soft. I do not have only one shape or size. I do not grow like the plants grow. I do not mind being changed into different looking objects, but it is not easy for people to change my shape. My shape cannot be changed without chipping away at me. What am I? (A rock or stone.)

Use Children's Literature

The Blue Willow, by Pam Conrad. In a traditional Chinese legend, King Shi Fair meets a local fisherman and falls in love. Tragedy results and the father learns he should have listened to his daughter. A blue willow plate is made to remind parents to listen to their children.

The Whales' Song, by Dyan Sheldon. Lily listened as her grandmother told her a story of the whales she loved as a child. She waited by the ocean with a gift for the whales, and finally they came to her bearing a gift of their own. Now it is Lily's turn to wait and listen for the whales.

Why Mosquitoes Buzz in People's Ears; A West African Tale, by Verna Aardema. When Iguana gets tired of listening to the mosquito tell his nonsense stories, he puts sticks in his ears so he can't hear anymore. Unfortunately, he does not realize that this creates so much chaos for the rest of the jungle creatures that the sun forgets to shine—and that is disastrous!

Welcome Home, Fergie! by Nancy Cocks. Fergie doesn't listen to his mother and suffers the consequences.

Use Music

Teach the skill of listening by clapping a pattern with your hands or snapping a pattern with your fingers. Ask the children to try and repeat the pattern. Make the patterns increasingly more difficult as the year progresses.

Play musical chairs. Teach the song "Are You Listening," created by Lynn Baker and sung to the tune of "Are You Sleeping?"

Are you listening? Are you listening?
I hope so! I hope so!
Can you sing the six steps?
Can you sing the six steps?
Ready, set, go! Ready, set go!

Stop what you're doing. Stop what you're doing.
Clear things away. Clear things away.
Turn toward the speaker. Turn toward the speaker.
Hear what they say. Hear what they say.

Think things over. Think things over.
Ask questions too. Ask questions too.
These are all the six steps.
These are all the six steps.
That I can do. That I can do.

Cut out a picture of a large ear. Pin the picture on the back of one chair. Put chairs in a circle. Begin to sing the song. When the music stops, the person who lands on the chair with the ear must recite the six steps of listening.

Listen for Clues

Put different objects inside film containers or small boxes. Ask children to shake the containers and try to figure out what is inside by the sound it makes.

Learn Listening Body Postures

Teach children effective listening body postures:

- Nod to let the speaker know you understand.
- Show your face to the person with whom you wish to speak.
- Raise your hand if you want to ask a question.
- Have a pleasant look on your face.
- Laugh with the speaker, not at the speaker.

Dramatize What You Hear

Read a story to the children. Invite them to act it out as a way of showing others how well they listened.

Effective Listening When Guests Speak

Idea submitted by Chris Broslavick and Tony Pichler. Invite students to use focused listening while a guest speaks on a topic of their choice. Use this format:

1. Review with students the six steps involved in the self-discipline skill of listening.

2. Introduce the guest speaker.

3. Invite the speaker to speak for no more than a minute per age of the group.

4. After the presentation, distribute paper and pencils to each student, or ask students to respond in their journals.

5. Invite the students to practice steps four and five of the skill of listening:

Step 4. Tell what you heard.

Step 5: Ask questions that are on the topic.

Direct them to write three sentences that describe what the speaker said and to list one question they would like to ask the speaker.

6. Share the responses with the class and the guest speaker.

7. Direct students to give themselves a score from 1 to 10, with 10 being high, to indicate how well they practiced their listening skills.

Matching Game

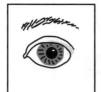

Listening Puzzle

1	STOP	STOP what you are doing or saying.
2		CLEAR AWAY distractions.
3		LOOK at or toward the person speaking.
4		ASK QUESTIONS if you do not understand.
5	I heard...	TELL what you heard.
6		DO what you hear the speaker say.

Game of Chance game board

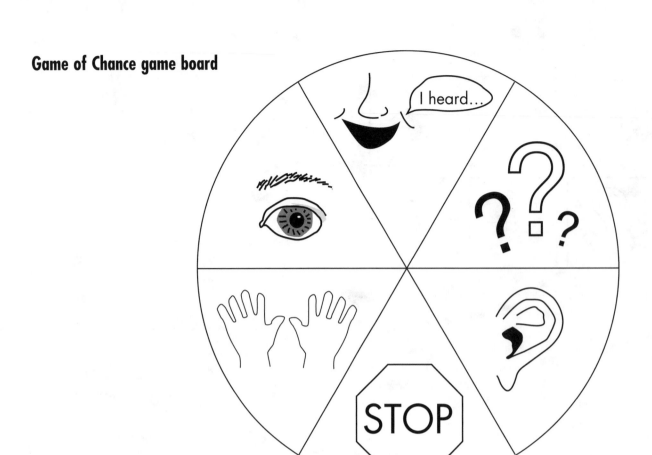

Decode the Message

What are the 6 steps of listening?

Use the decoder to find the answer.

<u>131</u> <u>250</u> <u>255</u> <u>159</u>,   <u>261</u> <u>110</u> <u>139</u> <u>654</u> <u>200</u>   <u>654</u> <u>80</u> <u>654</u> <u>169</u>

<u>33</u> <u>53</u> <u>131</u> <u>250</u> <u>200</u> <u>654</u> <u>261</u> <u>250</u> <u>53</u> <u>255</u> <u>72</u> <u>131</u>,   <u>110</u> <u>255</u> <u>255</u> <u>362</u>

<u>654</u> <u>250</u>   <u>255</u> <u>200</u>   <u>250</u> <u>255</u> <u>80</u> <u>654</u> <u>200</u> <u>33</u>   <u>250</u> <u>574</u> <u>139</u>

<u>131</u> <u>159</u> <u>139</u> <u>654</u> <u>362</u> <u>139</u> <u>200</u>,   <u>250</u> <u>139</u> <u>110</u> <u>110</u>   <u>80</u> <u>574</u> <u>654</u> <u>250</u>

<u>169</u> <u>255</u> <u>980</u>   <u>574</u> <u>139</u> <u>654</u> <u>200</u> <u>33</u>,   <u>654</u> <u>131</u> <u>362</u>

<u>400</u> <u>980</u> <u>139</u> <u>131</u> <u>250</u> <u>53</u> <u>255</u> <u>72</u> <u>131</u>,   <u>33</u> <u>255</u>

<u>250</u> <u>574</u> <u>139</u>   <u>250</u> <u>654</u> <u>131</u> <u>362</u>

(259 + 40) - 38	(36 + 25) + 19	68 + 91	(46 + 82) + 41	752 - (284 - 106)	725 - (282 + 304)	59 + 72	(752 - 284) - 106	(75-32) - 10
C	**W**	**P**	**Y**	**H**	**E**	**S**	**K**	**D**

826 - (32 x 18)	(3 + 7) x 98	75 - (32 -10)	(59 - 23) + 74	375 - (12 x 10)	(56 + 39) - 23	264 - (8 x 8)	(561 - 59) + 152	(15 + 5) x 20
T	**U**	**I**	**L**	**O**	**N**	**R**	**A**	**Q**

Different Ways to Listen

Appointment Card

❏ Focused listening: a self-discipline skill.

❏ Appreciative listening: when we listen to music or a story being read.

❏ Discriminative listening: when we distinguish facts from opinions.

❏ Comprehensive listening: when we try to understand the meaning of what is being said.

❏ Therapeutic listening: when we serve as a sounding board without passing judgment.

❏ Critical listening: when we listen and plan to evaluate when we heard.

This note entitles _____

to _____minutes of undivided attention. Please check the type of listening you need me to do as we work together.

Good Listener Certificate

Awarded to_____

for taking the time to be a good listener.

Given by _____

Date_____

I am not a planet.

1

You cannot see me in the night.

2

You cannot always see me in the sky during the day.

3

I don't help you stay very cool.

4

If you didn't have me you would be cold or damp most of the time.

5

What am I?

6

Following Instructions

This is how you are to make it. (Genesis 6:15)

Reflection: How do I help children follow God's plan for them, as Noah did?

The six steps to following instructions are

1. Practice good listening skills.

2. Repeat the instructions to myself or to someone else, or write them down.

3. List or say the first three things I need to do to begin the task.

4. Start on time.

5. Stay on task the entire work time.

6. Evaluate the task and how I followed instructions at the end of the work time.

Someone who follows instructions well

• Completes the task.

• Makes a plan.

• Uses time wisely.

• Knows what to do and how to do it.

• Knows how long it will take.

• Doesn't talk during instructions.

• Doesn't daydream or space out.

• Doesn't distract others.

GUIDED REFLECTION

FOLLOWING INSTRUCTIONS

As we begin our reflection, prepare to listen to a reading from Scripture. Close your eyes. Take a deep breath and feel your body relax. Feel your feet and legs relax. Notice your arms and head feeling heavy. Your breathing has slowed down.

Let's go back to a time many, many years ago. A man named Noah lived on the earth. He loved God very much and listened to God. He followed God's instructions when he heard God speak to him in prayer.

One day, God looked out over the earth and everywhere God looked he saw corruption and disorder. God noticed, however, that one man was still very, very good. With a sad heart, the Lord went to Noah and said, "I plan to destroy all life on the earth because it has become so evil. But, you I will save, and through you I will save animals of every kind."

Then, God said, "Make yourself an ark, Noah. Build it exactly as I tell you to build it. Take into the ark one pair of each animal that I tell you to take. Even if people wonder what you are doing and call you silly, continue to follow my instructions."

Noah followed God's command and built the ark just as God had told him to do. Picture Noah building the ark. What do you see? Where is he? How did Noah feel as he followed the instructions God gave him? Keep this image in your mind as you slowly open your eyes. Now take out your reflection booklet and draw a picture of anything you saw or heard during this reflection.

When most of the children have completed their illustrations, invite them to look at their pictures and describe what they saw or heard.

Engage in Discussion

Invite the children to think about the following questions.

- How long do you think it took from the time Noah heard God's instructions and the time he started to do them? Why do you think this?
- What do you think other people thought as they watched Noah following God's instructions?
- How do you think Noah felt following God's instructions?
- If Noah had not followed the instructions, what do you think would have happened?

Summarize the discussion by telling children how important it is for us that people like Noah were willing to obey God's commands. We are being asked now to listen and follow God's word, too. When we do we will be adding to the body of believers in the world and help others to believe.

Action Step

Each time you are given instructions today, think about Noah and how he followed God's word.

Tips for Teaching this Skill

There are three reasons why instructions usually are not followed:

- when people don't know what to do;

- when people don't know how to do it; and

- when people aren't motivated. They see no relationship between the task and themselves.

To help in this regard, cue the person to whom you are giving instructions to demonstrate the six steps of listening before you begin to give instructions. Avoid issuing an instruction without looking first to see if the person is ready to hear the message. Set a goal. Teach that much can be accomplished in a short period of time. Tell how long a person will have to work on a task. Negotiate with older youngsters by asking how much time they think they will need to finish what they are doing.

Teach Three Questions

Before allowing your children to begin work, coach them by asking three questions.

- Do you know what to do?

- Do you know how to do it?

- How much time will you have to complete the task?

Avoid the Pitfalls in Giving Instructions

These pitfalls can cause confusion and make it difficult for the children to correctly follow instructions.

1. Do not start one activity, move to another without finishing the first one, then return to the first one.

2. Neither should you stop one activity, start a new one, and then suddenly return to the previous activity.

3. Do not break the learning process by being distracted by an unrelated stimulus.

4. Do not dwell on an issue longer than necessary.

How It Works

A group of teachers visited an elementary school where children

---

Skill Reinforcement

Use these phrases throughout the year to help reinforce the skill of following instructions:

- There are three things I will ask you to do. They are: (list first, second, third, etc.).

- Does everyone know what to do?

- Does everyone know how to do the assignment?

- Does everyone have a plan on how you will begin?

- Did you set a goal for yourself during this time period?

---

had been learning about the fifteen self-discipline skills for several years. Each visitor spent about ten to fifteen minutes in a primary, intermediate, and junior high classroom. They were excited about the visit and had many good things to say during the lunch debriefing session.

One thing stood out in their minds: how kind the teachers were toward the junior high students. "What did you see or hear?" asked the facilitator of the group. "The teachers kept asking the students, 'How much time do you think you will need to finish this assignment?' or they would say, 'I can give you ten minutes to work on this project. Some of you may not finish, but do the best you can.'" The group had a long discussion about the benefits of delaying a child's impulsive need to begin work as soon as it is assigned. They liked the idea of waiting until three questions were asked and answered.

1. Do you know what to do? If not, this is a perfect time to ask every question you have about what you are to do.

2. Do you know how to do it? Who will be your partner, what materials will you need, etc.?

3. How long do you think you will need to complete the assignment?

As teachers built in a routine to help children wait and think before rushing through an assignment, they were doing as much as possible to help all the youngsters succeed in following instructions. This simple action demonstrated a most respectful attitude between student and teacher

19

Activities

Following Instructions in Daily Life

Take ordinary tasks that are done at school or home (for example, leave a classroom and go to the computer lab; make a peanut butter and jelly sandwich) and invite everyone to write down instructions on how these tasks can be accomplished. Experiment by exchanging instructions and following someone else's exactly as they are written. Discover why following directions is not always easy to do.

Practice Following Instructions

This idea was created by Rick Hook. Slowly read each item below. Invite people who wish to practice following verbal instructions to listen and then do what they think they heard you say. Have fun comparing the finished products. (See the illustration on page 24 for what the completed drawing should look like.)

1. Place a piece of paper lengthwise on a flat surface.

2. At the bottom of the sheet, draw two small squares approximately three inches apart.

3. Inside each square, across the bottom, draw a series of half circles.

4. Draw a large rectangle on top of and connecting both squares.

5. On top of the upper right corner of the rectangle, draw a circle whose diameter is the height of the rectangle.

6. If the circle were the face of a clock, draw a large S starting at the 5:00 position in the circle, extending it to the outside of the circle.

7. Draw another S parallel to the one just drawn about 1/8 inch away.

8. Draw another circle in the upper left corner of the first circle, half in and half out of the first circle.

9. In the upper left corner point of the rectangle, draw another S extending to the outside of the rectangle.

10. Just above the two parallel S's draw two ovals, one inside the other, the inner one being in the lower half of the outer one.

Evaluate Your Ability to Follow Instructions

Practice following instructions with children by involving their entire bodies in the exercise. Tell them to listen to what you say and when you finish speaking to do what they heard. Then create three simple instructions for them to follow, for example: "When I stop talking, I want you to get out of your chair; walk around the table three times; and shake hands with someone in the room. Please begin."

Use the same method with older children. Ask them how many instructions they would like to try and follow: four, five, or six. Let them self-evaluate when they are finished. Use a 1 to 5 point scale:

5 = Very good, I would change nothing.

3 = Somewhat good but not as good as it can be.

1 = Not very good. If I could I would like to try practicing the skill again.

Stand Up, Sit Down

This is an exercise that is fun in large or small groups. Once this is completed, older children can be challenged to write their own examples to be read aloud when people want to practice their ability to follow oral instructions.

Read the story below to children, but first give them these instructions: *Every time you hear a word that begins with the letter C stand up. Stay standing until you hear the word Jesus and then sit down. Stay seated until you hear another word that begins with the letter C, then get up. Continue this process until the story is finished.*

My Secret Hope

I've been a **Christian** all my life. I was baptized as a baby and my mother put a picture of **Jesus** in my room the day I was born. She says she wanted my room to be filled with **charity** and love, and that only **Jesus could** bring that much love. As I grew up I traded in my picture of **Jesus** with a big heart for one of him on the **cross**. This reminds me of the great love **Jesus** has for all people.

The picture of the **cross** keeps my secret hope alive. I know the power and love of **Jesus** can break down all the hatred and evil in the world. I know when I receive **communion** I bring **Jesus** into the world with me. I am then able to share my love with the people I meet. My secret hope is that I **can** tell everyone I meet about the work that **Jesus** is doing in the world.

Read and Follow Instructions

Enlarge and make copies of this exercise to distribute to your class.

This is a timed test. You have only three minutes to follow the instructions.

1. Read everything carefully before doing anything.
2. Put your name in the upper right hand corner of this paper.
3. Circle the word "name" in sentence 2.
4. Draw five small squares in the upper left hand corner.
5. Put an X in each square.
6. Sign your name under the title of this paper.
7. Put a circle completely around sentence number 7.
8. Put an X in the lower left hand corner of this paper.
9. Draw a triangle around the X you have just put down.
10. On the back of this paper, multiply 703 by 12.
11. Draw a rectangle around the word corner in sentence #4.
12. On the reverse side of this paper add 8950 and 9805.
13. Put a circle around your answer, and put a square around the circle.
14. Underline all even numbers in this test.
15. Now that you have finished reading everything carefully, do only instructions one and two.

Follow Instruction to Make Instructions

Give older students a chance to create their own card game by following a series of written instructions. Duplicate these and distribute to teams of five persons. There is no time limit on how long teams can take to complete this challenge.

Before working as a group, complete steps 1 to 4 individually.

1. Give each team 52 index cards. Each person should take 10 cards.
2. Each person places five index cards in the center of the table.
3. Each youngster thinks of a person from the Bible and writes the person's name on one of the cards. On two more cards write an event or activity that is associated with the person. On two more of the cards write a quote or teaching associated with the person.
4. Take the second set of five cards and repeat the process using a different person. Continue in this way until all 50 cards have been developed.

Work as a group to:

5. Lay out all the cards your team created. Place them face up so everyone can see them.
6. Study the cards for 3 minutes so you have a good idea of their contents.
7. After everyone has looked at them, pick them up. Shuffle them and give them to one person who will be the dealer.
8. Talk together and decide what the dealer should do with the cards to create a game. (Should he put them in the center of the playing surface? Should he deal 3 to 10 cards to each person? Should he deal cards to everyone else but not himself?)
9. Decide if the two blank cards will be used and how.
10. Play the game once.
11. Revise the game after talking about whether it was fair, fun, and challenging.
12. Play the game again as you make revisions.
13. When the game is fair, fun, and challenging, give your game a name or symbol.
14. Divide up the cards. Let each person write the name or draw the symbol on the back of each card to identify your deck.
15. Next, talk together and write instructions on how the game is played. Remember that someone else picking up the game for the first time will need to know:

- Title of the game.
- Objective: What should you try to do to win?

- Rules on how it is played.
- Creators of the game. List your names.

16. Wait until someone else in the room has also reached this point. Then, trade card games and play one another's games following the written instructions.

17. Make a written report to the other team about their game. List on a sheet of paper what you liked and what you disliked. Make suggestions about how the instructions might be improved.

18. Meet with the other team and share your ideas.

19. Go back to your original group and make any necessary changes the other team suggested.

20. Then redo any cards that are too difficult for others to read. Clean up your card game and the instructions. Place everything into a plastic bag.

21. Laminate some of the letter games. Place them in the game center to be used for review or shared with other grades. Other topics for the cards could include the Creed, the commandments, the sacraments, saints, and so on.

Practice Following Instructions

Gather seven colored crayons: blue, red, yellow, purple, orange, black, and green. Reproduce the worksheet found on page 24. Ask a youngster how many instructions he or she would like to be given at one time. Start with 1 or 2 and work up to 3. Slowly read each statement and invite the child to do what he or she hears you say.

1. Color the small circle blue.

2. Put a red X inside the large square.

3. Put a circle around the small triangle using a green crayon.

4. Make a number 2 inside the small rectangle with a yellow crayon.

5. Color the small triangle orange.

6. Print your name inside the large rectangle with a black crayon.

7. Draw a green triangle inside the large circle.

8. Put purple stripes inside the large triangle.

9. Put a red line under the small square and color this square purple.

10. Draw a yellow square around the small circle.

Let the children evaluate their performance in practicing the skill of following instructions by placing an A, B, C, D on the top of the page to indicate how well they practiced the skill.

Vary Classroom Instructions

Another option for practicing following instructions in a classroom is to vary the way you introduce assignments. These two starters can give new meaning to the phrase, "Let's begin our lesson." Instead of saying, "Take out your paper and put your name on it," try this: "Today I want you to practice following three instructions. Wait until you hear all three and then begin your work."

1. Write the name of the first book of the Bible on the top line of your paper.

2. Write the name of the person in the Bible who built the ark on the second line.

3. Print your first and last name on the third line.

Or:

1. Print your first and last name on the first line of your paper.

2. Draw a picture of our parish church using one-half of the paper.

3. Look up the meaning of the word "sacrament" in your textbook and write it down on the paper.

Make Procedure Booklets

Create a booklet entitled "The Way Our Class Does Things" or "The Way Our Family Does Things." Enlist the help of older students to prepare a checklist of instructions for any or all of the following activities.

1. Instructions a substitute teacher should know.

2. Instructions on how to welcome a new member of the class

3. Instructions on the care of a classroom or family pet.

4. Instructions on the steps to be taken to evacuate in case of a fire.

5. Instructions on how to behave during Mass.

6. Instructions on how to do chores.

7. Instructions most frequently given by adults.

The "I Forgot" Slip

This activity was created by Mary Jo Malm. Send home a letter similar to the one below. You'll find a sample copy of the "I Forgot" slip below.

Dear Parent,

This year your child will be working on the self-discipline skill of following instructions. To help children learn this skill I will be using an "I Forgot" slip.

There will be times your child may fail to bring necessary items to school or class. To remember to follow instructions overnight or from one week to the next can be a difficult skill for primary children. When your child forgets an item, the attached slip will be sent home. It will tell you the item he or she has forgotten and you will be asked to sign the form and send it back the following session. The form will be kept on file. At the end of each quarter, the forms will be returned to the children.

No one is punished or penalized if they have a large number of slips. Every child learns self-discipline skills at his or her own rate. The children will be competing only against themselves. They will be helped to reduce the number of slips they receive and tips will be provided on how this skill can be mastered.

You can help your child learn this skill by:

1. Refusing to bring the forgotten item up to school and allowing him/her to take the natural consequences of his/her actions.

2. Prompting your child to put the item near the front door.

3. Acknowledging that following directions over a long period of time is a difficult skill to learn. Everyone forgets things at times. Learning how to cope by using a system is often needed. So, you may want to practice the skill of following instructions at home with your own "I forgot" slip.

Sincerely,

Use Poetry

Adults give instructions many times throughout a day. Read the following poem to your children. Invite them to think about other instructions they have heard that are meant to teach them lessons about life. Challenge older children and yourself to create additional poems.

Beware of Coat Zippers

I have some information
That I think you all should know.
It has to do with zippers
On coats you wear for snow.
When the weather gets quite nippy
And the winds begin to blow,
Don't zip your coat up quickly
Or your tears will start to flow.
You will zip your lip, I tell you,
Or you'll zip your neck, Oh no!
Don't zip your coat up quickly
When you zip your coat, zip slow.

— Christine Marie Ryktarsyk

The "I Forgot" Slip

Date_____   Quarter 1__ 2__ 3__ 4__

Dear_____,

I forgot my _____ today. When I did not bring this item to school I was unable to follow instructions over a long period of time. I am working to get better at this skill. My teacher is helping me to practice and I know I can improve.

Student signature _____

Parent signature _____

Practice Following Instructions

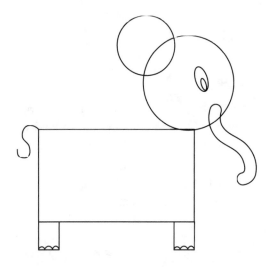

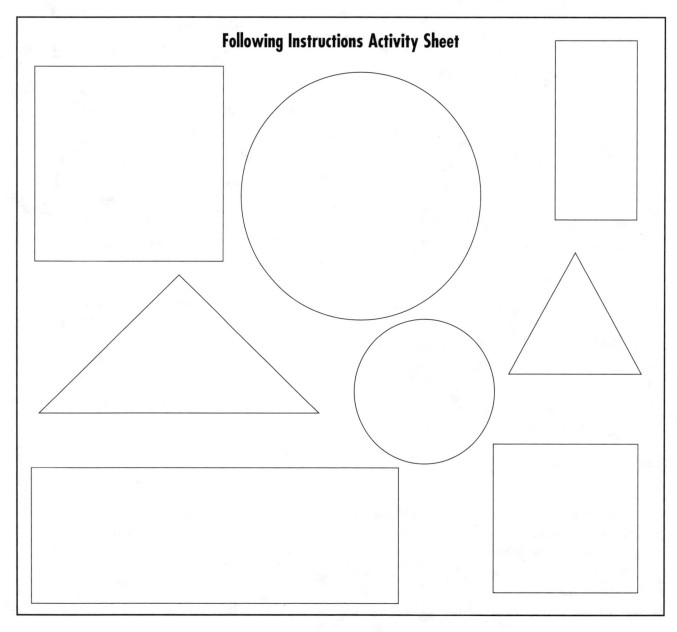

Following Instructions Activity Sheet

CHAPTER 3

Asking Questions

"Where is the child who has been born king of the Jews?" (Matthew 2:2)

Reflection: How do I teach children to use questions to deepen their faith, and be curious like the magi?

Good questions are questions that

1. Have not been asked before.
2. The speaker hasn't already told us about.
3. Other people might need answered too.
4. Will make the speaker feel comfortable and not ill at ease.
5. Help people think.
6. Keep the conversation on the topic.

People who ask good questions

- Use who, what, where, how, and why words to begin their sentence.
- Find out more information.
- Speak politely.
- Keep the conversation on track.
- Say "I don't know the answer but I'd like to."
- Don't ask questions that distract from the topic.
- Don't ask questions that have already been answered.
- Don't ask questions disguised as statements.
- Don't ask questions that are stallers.

GUIDED REFLECTION

ASKING QUESTIONS

As we begin our reflection, prepare to listen to a reading from Scripture. Close your eyes. Take a deep breath and feel your body relax. Feel your feet and legs relax. Notice your arms and head feeling heavy. Your breathing has slowed down.

Today we will journey back to the time of Jesus' birth. Mary, Joseph, and Jesus were all in a stable. In the stable were cattle and sheep. There was straw and a place for Mary to lay the baby Jesus.

In the distance, shepherds were guarding their sheep. All of a sudden a great light flashed down around them. They were frightened. An angel appeared to them and said, "Do not be afraid. I have wonderful news. This night a Savior is born for you. He is Christ the Lord. Go and see him." The shepherds listened and obeyed.

Now, in the East, there were wise men who studied the stars. They saw a bright star that they had never seen before, shining in the East. They left their homeland and moved toward the star. It led them to Jerusalem. When they arrived in Jerusalem, they had many questions. Listen carefully to what they are asking.

Did you hear them say, "Where is the baby who is to be your king? Where will the Son of God be born?" What else are they asking?

When you can hear two or three of their questions, slowly open your eyes. Now take out your reflection booklet and write down the questions. Illustrate what you saw.

When most of the children have completed their questions and illustrations, invite them to share their questions. They can then look at their pictures and describe what they saw or heard.

Engage in Discussion

- Write all shared questions on the board.
- Read the criteria for good questions to the youngsters and ask them to identify the questions that fit under each criteria. Mark the questions with the letters a, b, c, d, or e to indicate the criteria.
- Summarize the discussion by telling students how important it is for us that people like the Wise Men were willing to ask questions and were curious about their world. We can use the same criteria they did when we ask questions.

Action Step

Each time you are curious about something today, try to use the criteria for a good question.

Tips for Teaching this Skill

Asking questions is a basic self-discipline skill, which means that it will be difficult for children in kindergarten through third grade to do on their own without prompting.

When we ask questions, we wait for a speaker to finish speaking. We think: Am I curious about anything the speaker has said? How can I formulate my thoughts so I use the right words? Do I know the criteria for a good question?

Encourage questions by your posture and tone. Say, "Ask me every question you have about this topic," rather than, "Are there any questions?" Avoid asking questions that can be answered with one word, or "Yes" and "No." Allow wait time after asking a question. It is a good practice to tell youngsters you are counting to twenty before you acknowledge questions or answers. Count from one to seventeen quietly. Say, "Eighteen, nineteen, twenty" aloud, and then call on the persons who have raised their hands.

Questioning Techniques

Sometimes adults do not encourage children to practice the skill of asking questions because when children are practicing this skill, they do not always know how to do it well. Then adults feel trapped or stuck. You can show children that adults feel comfortable addressing most questions by using these techniques.

- "I'd prefer not to answer." If you do not want to answer questions or are unsure of the motive behind the question, ask: "What will you do with this information?" Or be more direct: "That's very personal. If you are serious about wanting to know, we can talk about it privately. When would be a good time for you to meet with me?"

- Pushing for an answer. When children push with questions and you don't want to debate or argue an issue, ask: "What do you want me to say?" or "What do you think?" or "You know how I think. What do you think I will say?"

- The last word. When someone always has to have the last word, or wants to continue a debate, throw the ball to them before you hit

your frustration point. Example: "Mark, why don't you have the last word on this issue. What did you hear everyone say?"

- Giving an answer that won't be liked. If you want children to know your answer may not correspond to what they want to hear, anticipate their discontent. "I'm going to say something now, and you may not like my answer. I hope you will be able to accept it and stop asking."

- *What if?* Middle grade youngsters love "What if..." questions. Many teachers post a long scroll of paper in the room. They title it "What if...." As these questions emerge, write the question on the scroll that is to be discussed throughout the month. Children can be invited to collect data and ask others outside of the school about the issue. Periodically set a time when new information or ideas can be discussed regarding the "What ifs..." that are listed on your scroll.

Five Types of Questions to Avoid

These types of questions should be avoided:

1. Questions you already know the answer to; for example, asking, "What did you do?" when you saw the action.

2. Questions that begin with "Why?" Children who have not yet developed a reflective way of thinking may not know why. Others are given an opportunity to make up reasons to avoid the consequences. It is better to state what you saw or heard and ask how something happened.

3. Questions that seem to put down the other person; for example: "Can't you do anything right?"

4. Questions that leave no options, such as ultimatums or questions that are unreasonable.

5. Questions that start with, "Would you like to…?" Middle grade and junior high students are too tempted to respond with a negative answer.

How It Works

When Miss Przybocki first started teaching the self-discipline skills, she used one lesson per week. Her second graders learned the six steps of listening and how to follow instructions. They made Hidden Skill booklets and recorded what they wanted to remember about the skill each time a new lesson was taught.

In addition, Ms. Przybocki made a flip chart for her class. Each time she taught a lesson she would illustrate or write key words or ideas that she intended to review many times during the school year. On one page of her flip chart she listed the criteria for a good question. With the children's help, the following items were identified.

A good question is one that:

• the speaker hasn't already answered;

• has not been asked before;

• other people would want answered too;

• begins with a "w" or "h";

• will not embarrass the speaker;

• is on the topic.

Ms. Przybocki used this flip chart whenever someone in the room celebrated a birthday. The child would be invited to take a place of honor in the classroom birthday chair. The birthday boy or girl would be asked ten questions by classmates. The questions had to fit the criteria for a good question. When all questions were asked and answered, the teacher invited the birthday person to tell the class one action step they would like the group to do ten times. One child wanted the class to rub their belly with one hand and the top of their head with the other ten times. Another child wanted the class to give the handshake of peace to ten students. Finally the class sang a birthday song to the student.

With a class of twenty-eight children, Miss Przybocki made certain that the self-discipline skill of asking questions was reviewed at least twenty or more times in one year. In addition, the activity was a pleasant one so the children associated practicing the skill with an experience they looked forward to.

Activities

Question Cards

To encourage children to ask questions, make stand-up question cards. On each card write one of these words: who, what, when where, why, what if, do, does, or can. Assign one card to two to three students. During a discussion, the children would be responsible for asking questions that start with the word on their card.

Too Many Questions

When children ask too many questions, help them distinguish between those they can answer for themselves and those they may need help with. Provide these children with six to eight question sticks each class. Place question marks on ice-cream sticks or cardboard strips. Tell the children that you will ask for one of the question sticks each time they need a question answered. Caution them to think carefully because many questions they will be able to answer for themselves.

When all of their sticks have been turned in, they will have to try to answer their own questions until it is time to distribute the sticks again. Determine the length of time that is appropriate to the developmental age of the child.

To Question or Not to Question

Help intermediate grade students determine which questions they can answer for themselves. Invite them to listen for one day and write down all the questions they hear their classmates ask.

At the end of the day, group youngsters in teams of three. Ask them to compare lists and write the ten most asked questions on newsprint. Let each group share what they heard. Then, challenge students to go through the list and circle all questions they think students should be able to answer for themselves. Invite volunteers to make a poster listing these questions. Hang the poster in a prominent spot for youngsters to begin monitoring the questions they ask.

Question Wheel

Using the example below, construct question wheels using cardboard and a metal spinner. Use the wheel to allow the children to interview one another when having a class or family meeting, or any other time when you want to engage in an organized discussion.

Question Wheel

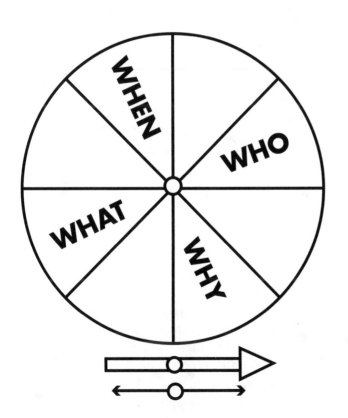

Use Stories to Teach about Questions

Read this story to the children:

A baby bird kept pestering a wise old owl with questions. "Why, he asked, "does the elephant have that long nose and those bulky legs, but mine are so small?"

"Don't bother me," said the owl.

"Why does the squirrel have such a soft, bushy tail and I don't even have that many feathers on my whole body?"

"Stop being a pest," said the owl.

"Why does the puppy chase after cats, but all I chase are other birds?"

"Be quiet, " said the owl.

"Why does the donkey have horns, but I don't even have tiny, stubby ones?"

"Stop it, I say," said the owl, in a very angry voice. "Don't bother me any more!"

"Why is it all the other grown-ups answer children when they ask questions, but you never answer me? You just say, 'Go away. Don't bother me.'"

"Because you don't really ask questions," said the owl quite seriously. "You just envy everybody else."

Now ask the children: what do you think the fable means? If the characters in the fable were people instead of animals, what questions would people ask? Some examples are:

• Why does my sister have beautiful blond hair and mine is so mousey brown?

• Why is Joe almost 6' and I am only 5' 7"?

• Why does Tonya's mother let her stay out past midnight and I have to be in by 11:00 PM?

Categorizing Questions

Give the children a copy of the riddle that follows. Invite them to ask questions that can be answered with a "yes" or "no" or "doesn't matter" response to try and solve the riddle. Keep track of the questions asked by writing them down on a piece of paper under the headings Yes, No, or Doesn't matter.

A Riddle

Every evening a man came home from work and entered the elevator in his apartment building. Every evening he pushed the button for the third floor, rode to the third floor, got off the elevator, and then walked seven flights to get to his apartment. Every morning he got on the elevator on the tenth floor and pushed the button for the ground floor. He rode down, then left his apartment building and went to work. How do you account for his strange behavior?

Allows children to ask questions until someone realizes that the man was very short and could only reach the lowest buttons on the elevator. Discuss together which questions helped the most to resolve the riddle.

Use Question Cubes

Develop a series of question cubes to help children learn words and categories that are related to their religion lessons. Use cardboard cubes 3" x 3" or 4" x 4" or wooden blocks for this activity. Place one word on each of the six sides of the cube. Invite the children to toss the cube. Use whatever word that appears on the top of the cube to ask a question. Topics can include the Bible, sacraments, saints, ten commandments, and prayer.

Birthday Celebrity

Follow a routine to celebrate birthdays, as Ms. Przybocki did in the story on page 28. Allow the birthday celebrity to sit in a birthday chair. Review with the class the criteria for asking good questions. Invite the children to ask ten questions of the birthday celebrity. Record the answers on a birthday celebrity sheet with the name of the person and a photo.

Question Box

Tell the children you will teach them about different kinds of questions we can ask about our faith. Print each question on the board or newsprint or on a flip chart. The following types of questions can be introduced.

1. Bible questions: Who led God's people out of slavery in Egypt?

2. Belief questions: What is the name of Jesus' mother?

3. Sacraments questions: Which sacrament makes us children of God and members of God's family?

4. Ten Commandments questions: Which commandment tells us not to fight, or injure anyone?

Display six to eight objects related to the above questions. Give children a chance to look at each one. Secretly place one object in a question box and remove all the others. Invite the children to select a category and ask a question that will help them determine the object that is in the box.

Using Poetry

Read the following poem to the students:

Where Are You Going?

Where are you going?
What's in the sack?
Why are you leaving?
Will you be back?

How will you get there?
Who's staying here?
Can you tell I'm afraid
By my eyes filled with tears?

When are you leaving?
Why can't you stay?
What will I do
While you are away?

I have one last question
To ask if you please...
Would you tell me you love me
Before you leave?

—Christine Marie Ryktarsyk

Invite students to discuss the possible answers to the questions posed. Older students might role play being the person in the picture and give answers to the questions posed by the younger child.

Now challenge youngsters to write a poem in which the first line is one of the following choices: a student keeps pestering a teacher; a child keeps pestering a parent; an employee keeps pestering his boss; a classmate keeps pestering another student; a parent keeps pestering a child.

CHAPTER 4

Sharing

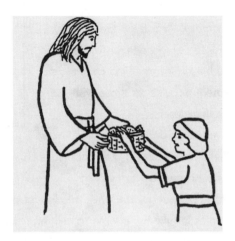

Then Jesus took the loaves, and when he had given thanks, he distributed them to those who were seated. (John 6:11)

Reflection: How do I help my students see that all gifts come from God and are meant to be shared?

There are four things we can learn to share

1. *Time.* Wait our turn. Begin tasks at once. Limit our conversations during group discussion time so others can talk too.

2. *Space.* Hallways, between desks or tables and common areas, playground, lunchroom, etc., are all places to keep neat so others can enjoy them too.

3. *People.* Teachers, friends, and loved ones need to be shared with others.

4. *Things.* Share limited resources and return things in good condition or the same way or better than we found them.

A person who shares

- Stays in their space.
- Uses their share of supplies.
- Works independently.
- Uses the appropriate tone of voice.
- Doesn't touch others or their things.
- Doesn't waste supplies.
- Doesn't rely only on the teacher.
- Doesn't use an outside voice when inside.

GUIDED REFLECTION

SHARING

As we begin our reflection, prepare to listen to a reading from Scripture. Close your eyes. Take a deep breath and feel your body relax. Feel your feet and legs relax. Notice your arms and head feeling heavy. Your breathing has slowed down.

Go back, back, back into your memory. Picture the time when Jesus was standing in the Sea of Galilee being baptized by John the Baptist. Shortly after his baptism, he began to travel the countryside preaching and teaching. He performed miracles for those with special needs. Many people began to follow Jesus.

One day, a flock of people followed Jesus and his disciples. When Jesus turned around, he saw that there were about 5,000 people. Jesus welcomed them. He talked to them about the kingdom of God and cured those who were sick.

Later in the day the people began to get hungry and they needed food. Jesus told the people to sit in groups of fifty. He then told the disciples to give the people something to eat. Where would the disciples find enough food to feed so many people? They looked and looked. They could only find five loaves of bread and two fish that a small boy had. The boy was taking the food home for his mother and sisters and brothers. But, when he knew Jesus was looking for food, the little boy gave what he had to Jesus. Jesus took the bread and fish and looked to heaven. He blessed the food. He broke the loaves and fish into pieces and put them into baskets. Then he told the disciples to pass the food to the people. Everyone ate until they were full. When they collected what was left, the little boy had more food than he had started with to take home to his family.

Picture the small boy in your mind. What did he do? How did the boy and Jesus feel about the things they had done? Keep this image in your mind as you slowly open your eyes. Now take out your reflection booklet and draw a picture of anything you saw or heard during this reflection.

When most of the children have completed their illustrations, invite them to look at their pictures and describe what they saw or heard.

Engage in Discussion

• Why do you think it was easy for the boy to give up the food he was taking to his family?
• Remind the children that everything we have in life has been given to us by God, and it is all meant to be shared. Talk about ways we can do this in our everyday lives.
• How can we act as Jesus did when he shared the loaves and fishes with the crowd?

Action Step

Each time someone asks you to share today, think of the little boy from the story above. He is our model for sharing.

Tips for Practicing this Skill

Sharing is working side by side with one or more persons, doing the same thing. It's a basic self-discipline skill, meaning it will be difficult for children in kindergarten through third grade to do on their own without prompting.

Primary-grade children learn to share time, space, people, and things. Intermediate-grade students learn to share responsibilities, information, cultures, and friends.

- When we share time, we wait our turn. We think: how am I going to use the time when it is my turn?

- When we share space, we wait until others have moved out of the space we wish to occupy, or until we can ask them to move. We think: how far can I count before it is my turn to get into that space?

- When we share people, we wait until the person is free to get their attention. We think: is there anything I can do to help myself while I wait?

- When we share things, we wait for others to finish using materials. We think: what condition will the object be in when I get it? How can I make sure I return it in the same or better condition?

When children receive gifts or something new there may be a time when they will not want to share. Protect their right to explore new items. Tie a ribbon or hang a sign on the object to let others know that this item is not yet ready to be shared. The person who owns the item should designate when it is time to let others use the object.

Skill Vocabulary

Use these phrases in class throughout the year to help reinforce the skill of sharing:

- Please get into your personal space.
- We will need to share the hallway as we go to class. I need three volunteers to show me what that will look like and sound like.
- This is your time. This is my time.
- Monitor your voice in the space we share.
- Please leave the room in a better condition than you found it.

How It Works

One afternoon two teachers drove onto a school lot and pulled up to the loading dock where they would have to unload boxes and materials for an upcoming workshop. They noticed two ninth-grade boys were using the space and a wall of the school building to practice their tennis game. As soon as the boys spotted the car, they left the area and walked about twenty-five feet away toward a fence. They looked a little guilty. The teachers thought maybe they weren't supposed to be in this area of the school grounds and were afraid they might get in trouble.

One teacher got out of the car and immediately went over to the boys. She reached out her hand and introduced herself. The boys shook hands and told their names. What came next was a total surprise to the two young 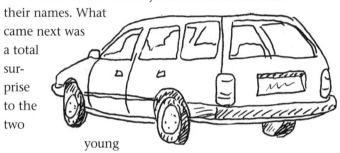 men. The teacher said, "We noticed when we drove up that you were playing tennis. We're sorry that we have to use this space and interrupt your game. We just want you to know it will only take us about ten to fifteen minutes to unload and then we will move the car."

The boys immediately said "Can you use some help?" "That would be super," said the teacher. When done together, the fifteen-minute job was reduced to five.

When the teachers left, they complimented the boys on their social skills, their willingness to share space, and their willingness to be of service to someone in need. "No problem," said one boy. "Glad to help," said the second. These two young men did not know about the fifteen self-discipline skills. They simply responded to an adult modeling the skills in action. The teachers took time to name for the boys the skills they had noticed them practicing. They used skill language in their conversation and identified how the boys' use of the skills was a help to others.

Activities

Share the Teacher

Teach children several picture cues that will help them to learn how to share the teacher. Enlarge the pictures found below and use them for classroom prompts.

- When you want the teacher's attention you should raise your hand and wait for your name to be called.

- If your teacher is talking to someone and you need attention, you can walk up to the adults and use the words "Excuse me." The adult will put up one finger to show you that she or he will be with you in a few seconds.

- If you cannot wait, there will be a bell or noise-maker on the teacher's desk that you can ring to alert everyone that there is an emergency.

- If your teacher is busy and cannot give you attention, you can go to someone in the room who is wearing an "I Can Help" button and request help from them.

Space Mats

Make the concept of sharing space more concrete for children. Give each child a large sheet of construction paper 2' x 3' and invite them to create a personal design on the paper. Laminate the mats when they are finished. Teach the children to bring this space mat with them when sitting in groups. The amount of space they should take up is defined by their personal space mat. A smaller version of the mat can be made for use at the lunch table or media center. Older youngsters might be invited to help make the space mats with the younger children.

Sharing Resources

Teach older students some principles of sharing materials.

- Recognize that there are limited resources.
- Ask permission to use items that are not yours.
- Commit yourself to work with others by waiting your turn to use an item.
- Use materials for a reasonable amount of time.
- Return the limited resource in the same condition you received it.
- If something happens, fix the item or offer to repay damages.
- Thank and appreciate others who were careful with limited resources.
- Put things back where you found them.

The Hunger Game

Another way to help children focus on sharing is through role playing. The "hunger" game is always very effective toward helping children experience the injustice that keeps poor people poor and hungry people hungry.

The game can be as elaborate or as simple as your circumstances allow. A simple version involves cookies, bread, and crackers. First set up three tables, each a little distance from the other. (If you don't have tables, simply mark three places on the floor.) On the first table place a large box of cookies; on the second a piece of bread; and on the third four crackers. (These amounts are based on a class of twelve children, so you need to adjust the numbers

for larger or smaller groups.)

Tell the children that you have brought them a snack and invite two of them to sit at the cookie table, three to sit at the bread table, and seven to sit at the cracker table. It won't take long for the children at tables two and three to object to the injustice of two children having a whole box of cookies! Ask them to work it out among themselves with Jesus as their guide. Ask what they think Jesus would do in this situation. The solution, of course, is for the children at table one to share their bounty, and for all three tables to pool their food supplies and share them. But sometimes children refuse to share, just as wealthy nations sometimes refuse to share with poor ones.

Talk about this experience afterward. Explain that a great many of the world's population have only "crackers" to eat. Some are more fortunate and they have "bread." But the smallest (and richest) group of people have all the "cookies." Questions you might pose include: In which group is our country? Is it fair that we have all the food we want while others go hungry? In what ways can we share with the poor?

What Do We Learn to Share?

Enlarge a copy of the sharing grid below. Challenge students to fill in words that begin with the letters share that would name times, spaces, people, things, and responsibilities that can be shared.

Sharing a Culture

Read the Vietnamese Tet Legend that follows. Discuss the legend using these questions.

- What can we learn about the Vietnamese from this story?

- Is the message about gift-giving contained in any American legends that we tell around the New Year?

- Do you know any legends from other countries that promote gift-giving involving things we cannot buy?

A Vietnamese Tet Legend

The Emperor Hung-Vuong told his twenty-two sons that the one who brought the most meaningful present to honor the gods of heaven and earth on New Year's Day would inherit the throne.

Twenty-one of the sons

Sharing Grid

	Time	Space	People	Things	Responsibilities
S					
H					
A					
R					
E					

went to far places to try to find precious gifts, but the youngest, Lieu, saw the ripe rice waving in the fields and felt it was so beautiful that nothing could be a more appropriate offering. So he asked his wife to make two special rice cakes, one round to symbolize the sky and one square to symbolize the earth.

When the princes came with their gifts of elephant tusks, rhinoceros horns, and other precious things, the emperor was pleased. When at last he came to the two simple rice cakes offered by Lieu and was told their meaning, he tasted them and was overwhelmed by their delicacy and simplicity. He shared them with his sons and all agreed the cakes were the most meaningful offering of the New Year.

Emperor Hung-Vuong named the round cake Banh Day and the square one Banh Chung. Since that day, the rice cakes have been traditional gifts given during Tet.

Challenge students to research and share information about another culture. Their report should include key words that help people understand the culture and the country where it is found. Students might want to include a story with a special meaning to that culture or country, and/or something concrete to help understand remember the culture or country.

Use Children's Literature

Lunch Bunnies, by Kathryn Lasky. Clyde befriends Rosemary on the first day of first grade. He was worried about carrying his own lunch tray until Rosemary drops hers and then he and the lunch lady share their time and help clean up.

Shoemaker Martin, based on a story by Leo Tolstoy, Brigitte Hanhart. Reprinted in 1997, this adaptation of a German fiction story by Leo Tolstoy tells about a Russian shoemaker who shares his things with three visitors one night and learns that Jesus visited him three times.

The Selfish Giant, by Oscar Wilde. It is always winter in the garden now that the giant will not allow children to play there. The selfish giant changes when his heart of stone is melted by a young boy who stands alone crying.

Third Grade Stinks! by Colleen McKenna. Gordie finally gets his favorite teacher in third grade, but Miss Tingle makes him share his locker with a girl instead of his best friend.

The Well: David's Story, by Mildred Taylor. During a drought in Mississippi in the early 1900's, David Logan's family shares their well water with both African-American and white neighbors, and resentment explodes.

Personal Space

Teach children that everyone has twelve inches of imaginary space around them. When they move, the space moves with them. They should try to stay within their own personal space. When they get too close to others, they invade their space. Everyone has a right to have his or her personal space honored by others.

Random space vs Orderly Space

Demonstrate for children how space can be conserved when things are orderly. Place a medium size box (with a lid) on the floor. Invite people to randomly toss one of their shoes in the box. Continue to fill the box as long as it can be closed with the lid. When as many people as possible have done this, take turns guessing how many shoes are in the box.

Then dump out the shoes. Invite the person who came closest to guessing the correct number to neatly order the same shoes in the box. If there is more space left, continue to add more shoes. When

finished, count the number of extra shoes that could fit in the box once they were neatly ordered. Draw conclusions about random use of space vs. orderly use of space.

Invite participants to investigate areas of the school and/or home that could be used more efficiently. Bring all suggestions to a future discussion and plan together how to make changes in spaces that need to be shared.

Use Music

Children can be taught more about sharing through music and gestures. The song below is sung to the tune of "Bingo."

Hidden Power Medley
By Jo Mersnick

S - H - A - R - E (to the tune of BINGO)

One HID - DEN POWER is how to SHARE, TIME
SPACE, THINGS, and PEO - PLE. S - H - A - R - E
S - H - A - R - E S - H - A - R - E We
All must learn to SHARE

(repeat)

verse 2	(clap) - H - A - R - E
verse 3	(clap - clap) - A - R - E
verse 4	(clap - clap - clap) - R - E
verse 5	(clap - clap - clap - clap) - E
verse 6	(clap - clap - clap - clap - clap)

Sharing Can Have Different Meanings

Idea submitted by Chris Broslavick and Tony Pichler.

Divide the class into groups of three. Distribute an envelope to each group. The envelope should contain:

- a paper circle about 3" in diameter
- a 5" paper square
- a paper triangle whose longest side is 4"
- two pieces of string, each 54" long
- a pair of scissors
- a ruler.

Instruct one child in each group to take a piece of string from the envelope and share it equally with the other two students in the group. Then ask a second student to give each person in the group either a paper circle, a square, or a triangle from the envelope.

The final person in each group should take the second piece of string from the envelope and cut it long enough to go around the circumference of each person's paper object. Then discuss these or similar questions:

- What is your observation about the length of the first piece of string?
- What is your observation about the second piece of string?
- * What can be done to share the resource of the string more equitably?
- If we tie the pieces of string together, what possibilities emerge?
- In our own lives, how can we share more fully with those who have less than we do?

Summarize the exercise by reading Luke 11:5–13 and emphasizing that sharing can mean we get equal parts. It also means that everyone should have what is sufficient for their needs.

Faith Sharing

Idea submitted by Chris Broslavick and Tony Pichler.

Begin by quieting the group. Light a candle and place it in an appropriate setting. Share a short prayer, such as this:

Jesus said, "I am the light of the world.... Whoever follows me will have the light of life and will never walk in darkness" (John 8:12). Lord Jesus, you also said that where two or three come together in your name, you are there with them. The light of this candle symbolizes your presence among us. We begin our faith sharing tonight with a Sign of the Cross to remind us that not only are you present, but the Father and Spirit as well. *Have everyone make a Sign of the Cross.*

Invite a volunteer to read Acts 2:42–47. Following the reading, invite the children to reflect on the words they have just heard. They can do this silently, or they can write down their thoughts.

After a few minutes, ask the students to share their thoughts with the rest of the group. When all who so desire have had a chance to speak, read the passage to the students again. This time, instead of focusing on a particular phrase, word, or idea, instruct them to try and understand the meaning of the passage in its entirety. Again, after a period of reflection, ask everyone to share their thoughts.

Conclude this faith sharing with a group recitation of the Lord's Prayer.

CHAPTER 5

Social Skills

A woman named Martha welcomed him into her home. (Luke 10:38)

Reflection: How do I help my students act as faith-filled Christians?

Having good social skills means

1. Using table manners.

2. Saying please, thank you, and excuse me.

3. Dressing appropriately.

4. Attending to personal hygiene.

5. Giving and receiving compliments.

6. Using greeting and leaving skills.

7. Helping visitors and newcomers feel welcome and comfortable.

A person with good social skills

• Uses good manners and is polite.

• Makes others feel comfortable.

• Thinks of the needs of others.

• Isn't rude.

• Doesn't embarrass others.

• Doesn't think only of himself or herself.

GUIDED REFLECTION

SOCIAL SKILLS

As we begin our reflection, prepare to listen to a reading from Scripture. Close your eyes. Take a deep breath and feel your body relax. Feel your feet and legs relax. Notice your arms and head feeling heavy. Your breathing has slowed down.

Picture Jesus sitting very comfortably on a hill. Once again people were all around him. He was telling them a parable. He helped cure the sick. He prayed with people who were victims and were suffering. Finally, it was time for him to continue his journey. He got up and started to walk on the dusty roads.

Jesus entered a village where he had special friends. A woman named Martha was there with her sister Mary. When Jesus came to their house, Mary and Martha welcomed Jesus. They hugged him and smiled broadly when they saw him. They asked him to remove his dusty sandals and gave him water and a cloth to clean his feet.

When they invited him to sit down, Mary chose to sit beside Jesus. She listened to everything he had to say. Martha was busy in the kitchen, worrying about what she would give Jesus to eat and drink. Jesus enjoyed his visit with his two close friends. He was sad when he had to say goodbye to them.

Think about what Martha and Mary did. What was the first thing they did when they met Jesus? Keep this image in your mind as you slowly open your eyes. Now take out your reflection booklet and draw a picture of anything you saw or heard during this reflection.

When most of the children have completed their illustrations, invite them to look at their pictures and describe what they saw or heard.

Engage in Discussion

• Ask your youngsters to give examples of their parents' words and actions when guests come to their house or when they meet someone new.

• On the board, make a list of other social skills the children think are important.

• How can we develop friendships as Jesus did with Martha and Mary?

Action Step

Invite youngsters to make a list of all the social skills they see or hear for the rest of the day. Ask them to share the list five minutes before the end of the day.

Tips for Practicing this Skill

Social skills are rules that help people relate to one another in a positive way. Using social skills is a basic self-discipline skill, meaning it will be difficult for children in kindergarten through third grade to demonstrate on their own without prompting.

When we use social skills, we wait until we have noticed another person. We think: How can I make this person feel comfortable and at ease? What social skills can I show?

Teach the children that if they choose to use a social skill, there will be a benefit to themselves as well as for others.

How It Works

Anxious about how a student who had invited a guest speaker to class might use her social skills, a teacher had this conversation.

Teacher   "Bess, I know you will be introducing Mr. Rockwell to our class on Thursday, and I was wondering if you have ever done this before."

Bess   "No."

Teacher   "Well, I'd like to review with you some actions other people do when they introduce speakers. If you hear anything you think you can use, please feel free to take notes. Would that be all right with you?"

Bess   "Sure."

Teacher   "Let's just picture how this will go. Where did you tell the speaker you would meet him?"

Bess   "He will come to the school office, and I will meet him there."

Teacher   "When you meet Mr. Rockwell, it will be expected that you introduce yourself and also get his full name, to make sure you are bringing the right person down to our room. Have you thought about how you will do this?"

Bess   "I will say, 'Hi my name is Bess.'"

Teacher   "Remember to reach out your hand and shake his as you give him both your first and last name. You may want to find out if he has ever met the principal. If not, you might want to introduce him to her.

> ## Skill Vocabulary
>
> Use these phrases in class throughout the year to help reinforce social skills:
>
> • When you choose to show a skill there will always be a benefit to yourself and others.
>
> • Using your social skills is one way to make others feel good (e.g., important, noticed, recognized)
>
> • What if everyone decided to do this action?
>
> • What if no one ever did this action?
>
> • Is there a custom we can honor? Should we make changes?
>
> • What would you like someone to do for you in this situation?

On your way from the office down to our classroom, have you thought of what you will talk about?"

Bess   "Well I have an uncle who works with him and I thought I would talk with Mr. Rockwell about him."

Teacher   "That would be good. Networking is always important. You may meet other teachers along the way and it would be good to introduce him to them."

Bess   "I never thought of that."

Teacher   "When you get to the classroom, how will he want the room arranged for his talk? Will he bring a resume for you to use when you introduce him? What will he want you to say about him?"

Bess   "I'd better take some of these things down on paper."

The conversation continued until the ten minutes were up. Mrs. Cardwell gave Bess a hall pass and the meeting ended. Bess did an outstanding job of escorting Mr. Rockwell to the room and introducing him without making jokes or nervously laughing. On her own initiative, she bought a thank-you card and invited everyone in the class to sign it on the following day. Bess had a chance to practice a social skill she had never done before. Mrs. Cardwell was saved from a potentially embarrassing situation, and everyone had a good learning experience.

Activities

Learning to Say Thank You

There are three times when children should be taught to say thank you:

- when someone gives you something;
- when someone does something for you;
- when someone compliments you.

Use this card to help the students keep track of their use of this skill

---

Thank You Card

Name_____

Make an X on a line each time you hear someone say, "Thank you," or you say these words.

___	___	___	___
___	___	___	___
___	___	___	___
___	___	___	___
___	___	___	___

Saying Excuse Me

Here is a checklist for helping children recall times when it is appropriate to say "Excuse me." Students can use this to role play the right way and the wrong way to say "Excuse me."

Five times when you should say "Excuse me":

- ❑ when you need to interrupt;
- ❑ when you need someone to move out of the way;
- ❑ when you want to leave the table while eating;
- ❑ when you accidentally bump into someone;
- ❑ when you make an impolite sound. (Note: Impolite sounds are those that could be offensive to another person.)

Interactive Posters

Cut ten strips of paper three inches by one inch to make rays for a sun. Glue a velcro circle on the back of each strip. Laminate the strips so that a marker will wipe off and they can be reused. Write the social skill words and actions the children will be practicing that day or during the week on the strips of paper.

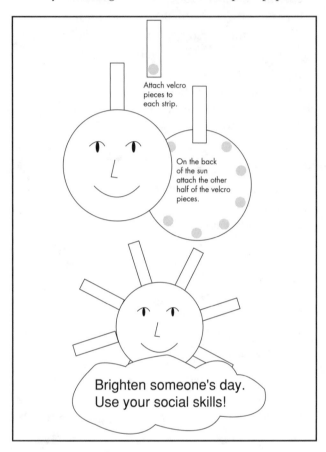

Design a poster with a blue cloud and yellow sun like the one shown above. Print this caption at the bottom of the poster: Brighten Someone's Day. Use Your Social Skills! Glue velcro circles along the outer edge of the sun. Each time one of the social skill words is said in context or actions done without a reminder, place the strip with that word or action

on the sun to complete the picture. At the end of each day gather the children around the poster and discuss their progress.

Illustrate Social Skills

Invite the children to illustrate the social skills they think are important to remember. When they are completed, hang the pictures on a bulletin board or arrange them around the classroom. Invite students from other classrooms to view the posters and listen to your students explain their illustrations.

Greeting and Leaving

Teach children the words used in other countries when greeting and leaving. Practice a different greeting each day of the week.

LANGUAGE	HELLO	GOODBYE
Spanish	Hola	Adios
Russian	Priviyet	Dobre Vetcher
Italian	Buongiorno	Arrivederci
French	Bonjour	Au revoir
Japanese	O Ha Ya O	O Ya Su Mi
Korean	On Yun Ha Say Yo	On Yo Ge Say Yo

Table Etiquette

Teach young people some rules of table etiquette as part of their social skills.

- Do not reach across the table for something. Say, "Please pass the _____."
- Talk quietly with the people seated near you. Take turns talking.
- Unfold your napkin and place it in your lap before you start eating.
- Say "Excuse me" when you must leave the table.
- Once you touch a piece of food, take it and put it on your plate.
- When you are done eating, fold your napkin and lay it on the table.
- Chew with your mouth closed and do not speak with food in your mouth.
- Don't fight at the table.
- Wash your hands before eating.
- Don't put your elbows on the table.

Greeting Others

Find opportunities for children to practice the social skills that they are learning. Discuss the steps that follow. Invite the students to report on the new people they meet and the steps in this format they feel comfortable using.

- Stand in front of the person to be greeted. (Avoid shouting or standing at the side to make it difficult to see one another.)
- Reach out your right hand.
- Take the hand of the other person and gently shake it up and down.

- Say to the person, "My name is _____." (Use your first and last name if you are meeting someone for the first time.)
- Listen when the person tells you his or her name.
- Use the person's name if you want to ask a question or have time to visit.
- When you are ready to leave one another, say, "I'm glad I met you," or "I hope we meet again."

The Three Cs of Social Skills

When children have mastered the basic social skills, they can be helped to determine for themselves when a social skill is needed, and what that action might be. Teach students in grade five and up to use the three Cs—custom, courtesy, and common sense— to help determine what action would be appropriate.

- *Custom (addresses the past)*. Is there a custom or tradition that others have done before? Can I honor the custom? Should I change or modify it?
- *Courtesy (addresses the present)*. If I were in this situation, what would I like someone to do for me?
- *Common sense (addresses the future)*. What would happen if no one ever did this action? What would happen if everyone did this action?

Finally, students can ask this question:
- How would Jesus act in this situation?

Role Play

Children often have questions about how they should act or respond in social situations. To help in this regard, students can role play different situations, for example:

- going to someone's house for the first time;
- attending church;
- going on a trip with a neighbor;
- attending a funeral service;
- visiting aging relatives;
- attending social situations without a family member;
- giving and receiving compliments;
- how to respond when given an honor or award;
- the use of RSVPs.

Telephone Manners

Discuss the list of telephone manners that many families use. Talk about each and make modifications until you have develop your own preteaching checklist.

- Telephone conversations, unless an emergency (life/death situation) will last no longer than ten minutes each for all members of the household.

- When answering the phone, give a greeting and your name to let the caller know he/she has reached the correct party.

- When calling someone to the phone, wait until you can see the face of a person before telling him/her the phone call is for them. Avoid yelling for the person who is wanted.

- A message pad and a pen or pencil will be placed by the phone at all times so messages can be taken.

- Ask the caller how to spell names, addresses, etc. Repeat information back to verify it is correct.

- When someone is using the phone, avoid making loud noises or disturbances.

Television Social Skills

Poll students to discover two or three of their most frequently watched, half hour T.V. shows. Select one show and video-tape it. Schedule a time when the class can watch the show. Decide before the show begins who will observe the following:

1. How courteous are the people on the show toward one another? Do they greet each other? Do they say, "Please" and "Thank You"?

2. What are their eating habits and table manners like?

3. What are the non-verbal facial expressions, body posture, and eye contact, given or not given by members of the show?

4. How is humor used? Does it put others down, or build them up and make them feel good?

5. What is the attitude towards persons who are from different cultures or traditions?

At the end of the viewing, discuss what was observed. Write a letter to your local newspaper sharing your observations with the entertainment editors. Challenge the students to do a similar experiment at home with their family.

Bullying: A Negative Social Behavior

Bullying can be found in two types of behaviors.

- Direct behavior, that is, teasing, taunting, threatening, hitting and stealing that are started by one person against another.

- Indirect behavior, that is, spreading rumors that cause another person to feel excluded or isolated.

To be considered bullying the behavior must occur repeatedly over time. The victim must feel it is an ongoing pattern of harassment or/and abuse. Physical assault as a form of bullying is easiest to curb. Verbal abuse is harder to stop. Bullies are often people who think that physical punishment or hitting others is a way to handle problems. They often are defiant toward authority and break rules. Bullying in school years can lead to legal or criminal troubles as adults. Victims of a bully rarely defend themselves when confronted. They need peers who will befriend them and help them feel part of a group.

CHAPTER 6

Cooperation

They signaled their partners in the other boat to come and help them. (Luke 5:7)

Reflection: How do I help my students establish a community that shows we are all one in Christ?

When we cooperate, we

1. Recognize there is a job to be done.
2. Are able to tell the goal.
3. Brainstorm ideas to reach the goal.
4. Agree on a strategy and assign tasks.
5. Complete my share of the task on time.
6. Talk about how the group accomplished the task.
7. Make recommendations on the strategies that helped or hindered cooperation.

A person who cooperates

- Focuses on a group goal.
- Does his or her fair share.
- Offers to help if someone needs it.
- Doesn't work against the group.
- Doesn't let others do all the work.
- Doesn't think only of his or her own needs.

GUIDED REFLECTION

COOPERATION

As we begin our reflection, prepare to listen to a reading from Scripture. Close your eyes. Take a deep breath and feel your body relax. Feel your feet and legs relax. Notice your arms and head feeling heavy. Your breathing has slowed down.

Picture in your mind a beautiful, calm blue lake. You and your friends have nets, poles, and bait. You are looking for a great spot to fish. You pack a boat and carefully select a spot that looks perfect. The leader of your group is a boy named Simon. You set out and fish all night.

It is almost morning when you come back to shore. You have had no luck catching fish. You are tired, worn out, and very hungry. Simon is very discouraged. When you reach your camp on the shore, you see a man talking to a group of people. He sees you and when your eyes meet you recognize him. He says to you, "Go back into the deep water and lower your nets for a catch." Simon tells his Master, "We have worked hard all night and have caught nothing. But if you tell us to go, we will lower the nets again."

When we go back into the boat and throw out our nets, we are surprised. A great number of fish have come into our nets. There are so many fish that our nets are tearing. The effort needed to bring in the catch is too great. We signal to the others to come and help us. They rush over with their boats to help us gather in all the fish.

Visualize this scene in your mind and keep this image in your mind as you slowly open your eyes. Now take out your reflection booklet and draw a picture of anything you saw or heard during this reflection.

When most of the children have completed their illustrations, invite them to look at their pictures and describe what they saw or heard.

Engage in Discussion

• How did the people in this story cooperate with one another?
• Who do you think the person was on the shore? Why do you think so?
• Remind the children that Jesus told the apostles he would make them "fishers of men." What would the apostles have to do to cooperate with Jesus?
• How can we learn to cooperate with one another as the apostles did with Jesus?

Action Step

Each time someone asks you to cooperate today, think of Simon and his companions. Will you choose to practice this skill like they did?

Tips for Practicing this Skill

Cooperation means to work and act with others for the good of everyone. In the Native American culture several people use a stick to beat the drum. Unless each person plays the required rhythm the intended music cannot be heard.

Cooperation is a constructive self-discipline skill, meaning it will be difficult for children in kindergarten through grade six to demonstrate on their own without prompting. When we cooperate, we wait for everyone to complete their portion of a task. We think: can I help anyone else? Is my portion the best it can be? Can I make improvements?

The foundation of this skill starts when children learn to share. Sharing is working side by side doing the same or similar task. Cooperation means working side by side (or away), working on different tasks in order to complete a project that requires everyone's individual activity.

Children can be taught to work in teams of four to five in cooperative learning groups. Invite youngsters to select how many people they would like to work with during some of the cooperative activities. Discuss with your students what it takes to cooperate.

1. Each person must decide to do their best.

2. Every person is important in order to get the task done.

3. We can offer to help if help is needed.

4. We can ask for help if we need it.

Skill Vocabulary

Use these phrases in class throughout the year to help reinforce cooperation:

• When we cooperate, everyone must do their unique part to accomplish the task.

• Are you ready to cooperate, even if the end result is different than you want it to be?

• Remember you are working as a team. Teammates help one another.

• Can someone else help you?

• Can you help someone else?

• Let's brainstorm ideas.

• How can I help you get started?

How It Works

Bo was a sixth grader. He was in a school were the fifteen self-discipline skills had been taught for four years. All the children were learning information about the skills and were practicing the skills they needed to become more grown-up.

On this particular day, the youngsters were asked to name one skill that they felt they had mastered and one that was a challenge for them. Bo told the class how asking questions was an easy skill for him, but cooperation was difficult. "I don't cooperate at home and I don't cooperate at school." he said. His classmates chuckled because they knew Bo had spoken the truth.

The teacher thanked him for sharing that information, then added, "Cooperation is a difficult skill for some people to acquire without help. I don't know when you will decide to practice the skill. I hope it will be sometime in the near future because you will need that skill the rest of your life." Bo listened and accepted the comment.

A short time later, an assignment was given to the class, and the teacher noticed that Bo was the first one finished. "Would you please pick up the papers as your classmates finish this assignment?" the teacher asked Bo. "Yes ma'am," he said, and quietly moved around the room picking up the completed papers.

When the teacher looked up, she noticed that Bo had not returned to his place, even though all of his classmates had finished their assignment. She looked around the room and found Bo at a side table, sorting the papers so all the headings were top side up. When the stack of papers was perfect, Bo handed the completed stack to his teacher. "Oh, Bo," the teacher said with much feeling. "About twenty minutes ago you told us that cooperation was a difficult skill for you to do, but just now, by your actions, you showed us what that skill looks like."

Several of Bo's classmates overheard the comment, and began to clap. "Bo just practiced cooperation!" one of them said. With that, the entire class gave Bo a round of applause. Bo learned a very important lesson that day: some people will be good at some skills and not so good at others. When we want to get better, we just have to practice.

Activities

Illustrate Cooperation

Ask children to write about or illustrate a time when they were involved in the skill of cooperation. The picture or story should include these components:

- more than one person working on a task;

- each person being assigned a different job;

- the task couldn't get finished unless each person did their part.

Cooperate to Complete a Puzzle

Divide a group of people into teams of four to five members. Obtain a 75 to 100 piece puzzle to be given to each group. Before introducing this exercise place an equal number of puzzle pieces in plastic bags so each member of the group will have approximately 15 to 20 pieces. Ask each group to record their prediction of how long it might take them to finish the puzzle. Then, allow time for them to work. When finished debrief using the following questions:

- How close did you come to your prediction?

- What were some of the challenges in cooperating to finish the puzzle?

- How would you rate the group's participation of the task? How would you rate your own participation of the task? (Use a scale of 1 to 5, with 5 indicating the greatest amount of participation.)

Puzzle It Out

To create this cooperative learning exercise

1. Cut 5 six-inch squares of poster board. Then cut each square as shown in the diagram. Put letters on the pieces as shown.

2. Place the pieces in five different envelopes marked as shown on the diagram.

3. Form teams of five players each.

4. Give each person one envelope.

5. Instruct the groups that the object of this exercise is for each person in a group to create a six-

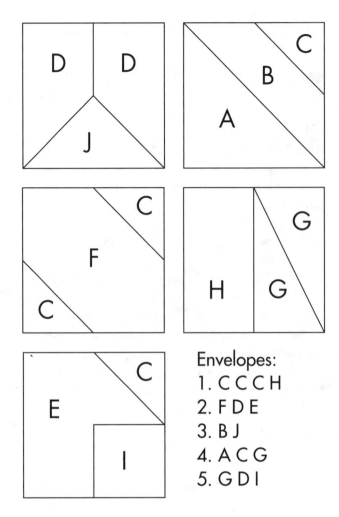

Envelopes:
1. C C C H
2. F D E
3. B J
4. A C G
5. G D I

inch square out of the shapes. No envelope contains the right shapes to complete this project. You must cooperate to succeed.

6. For the first five minutes participants

- may not speak to one another;

- may look at other pieces but may not take any;

- may slide a piece over to another person or to the middle of the table, but may not fit it in place for anyone.

7. For the next five minutes participants can communicate verbally with one another and practice cooperation.

8. When the time is up, discuss the experience using these three questions:

- What were some of your personal thoughts and feelings as you practiced the skill of cooperation?

- What were some things that helped your group finish the task?

- What are some of the other times when you have to practice cooperation?

Cooperation Journal

Using the steps of cooperation, invite each member of the class to set a personal goal for one week to practice the skill. Invite them to keep a personal log in which they record two times during the week when they chose to cooperate. Duplicate the following questions so each person has a copy to use for reference.

Practicing Cooperation

- I noticed, or someone I was with noticed, that a task needed to be done and it would take more than one person to do it. What did you notice?

- Describe what you decided needed to get done. What was the goal?

- List the actions or jobs each person was assigned.

- How much time did it take?

- On a scale of 1-5 (5 being the best rating), what rating would you give to the completed task? Why?

- What suggestions do you have that would have made this cooperative adventure more successful?

Chores Equal to Your Age

Cooperation in a family means children take on the responsibility for doing a number of tasks equal to their age. When asked to list the fourteen tasks they might be responsible for in their home, a group of eighth graders generated this list.

1. Take out the garbage.

2. Help with dishes and clearing the table.

3. Care for animals or pets.

4. Clean my room.

5. Dust and vacuum.

6. Do homework and show it to parent(s).

7. Lawn care including mowing, trimming trees and bushes.

8. Respect family members, by respecting the privacy of others and not using back talk.

9. Help with laundry.

10. Get myself up in the morning.

11. Pick up shoes and clothes. Ask everyday if I can help with any chore.

12. Don't argue after an appropriate reason has been given.

13. Say "I love you" every day.

14. Look for a good TV show for the family to watch.

Ask your students to list activities that they are each expected to do in their families.

Brainstorming

When people work cooperatively together, the technique known as brainstorming is frequently used so that everyone feels they have contributed to the discussion. To practice this technique, select a topic for discussion. Introduce the following steps of brainstorming to your students. Use these to arrive at a conclusion or solution to the topic being discussed.

Rules of Brainstorming

1. All ideas are significant and will be recorded. (List ideas on a blackboard or flip chart. Invite children to make their own list in their notebook.)

2. Everyone can have equal time to explain their ideas.

3. The ideas will be evaluated according to certain criteria: reasonableness, time, cost, and what will be taught or learned.

4. The group will come to a consensus on the idea that is selected.

5. The best idea will be one that incorporates as many points of view as possible.

Use Children's Literature

Enhance children's understanding of how cooperation looks and sounds in action by reading one or more of the following books aloud.

Angel Child, Dragon Child, Michele Surat. Ut does not like her new American school. The other children laugh at her. She misses her mother who is still in Vietnam. A boy Ut dislikes figures out how to reunite them, and Ut discovers the skill of cooperation.

Ox-Cart Man, Donald Hall. This story is about the spirit of cooperation that prevails in many Quaker families. Each member of the family has responsibilities that are integral to the family's survival. Caldecott Medal 1980.

Drummer Hoff, Barbara Emberley. Winner of The Caldecott Medal, 1968, this book shows how many people it takes to complete a single task.

It Takes a Village, Jane Cowen-Fletcher. All the people from the African village take part in looking after Kokou at the market. Yemi is happy to look after her younger brother but soon learns responsibility is equally and proudly shared by all in the village.

Use Music

Children can be taught about the self-discipline skill of cooperation through music. You can start by teaching them the song below.

Hidden Power Medley

By Jo Mersnick

COOPERATE
To the tune of "When Johnny Comes Marching Home"

When there is a job that we must do, CO - OP - ER - ATE.

Make up a team and work it through, CO - OP - ER - ATE.

A - gree and del - a - gate, Talk and plan, Work to - ge - ther

and say "We can!" and we'll get the job done when

we all CO - OP - ER - ATE. Re - mem - ber E - val - u - ate,

When fin - ished we'll Cel - e - brate. Yeah! (spoken)

CHAPTER 7

Understanding the Reasons for Rules

"Child, why have you treated us like this? Look, your father and I have been searching for you in great anxiety." (Luke 2:48)

Reflection: How do I help students understand God's laws and how to follow them?

When we understand the rules we

1. Know the rules and can recite them to others.

2. Ask someone when we don't understand the rule or the reason for the rule.

3. Choose to follow the rule even if we don't feel like doing so.

4. Teach the rules to younger persons or others who do not know the rules.

5. Use the right process to suggest changes to the rule if we don't like it or agree with it.

Someone who understands the reasons for rules

• Is able to follow rules.

• Chooses to follow rules.

• Can tell the reasons for rules.

• Can work to change rules.

• Doesn't complain without taking action.

GUIDED REFLECTION

UNDERSTANDING THE RULES

As we begin our reflection, prepare to listen to a reading from Scripture. Close your eyes. Take a deep breath and feel your body relax. Feel your feet and legs relax. Notice your arms and head feeling heavy. Your breathing has slowed down.

Picture in your mind Joseph and Mary and Jesus riding in a caravan. The roads they travel are dusty, and dirt flies up as they make their way to Jerusalem. It is Passover time, a time for celebration. After spending several days in Jerusalem, Mary and Joseph begin the long journey back home. Although Jesus is not riding with them, they are certain that Jesus is with some of his other friends and relatives farther back in the caravan.

When the caravan makes the first stop, Mary and Joseph begin to look for Jesus among the other people. They search and search. When they cannot find him, they begin to get very anxious. They think perhaps they have left him behind, so they turn around and go back to Jerusalem.

They look for their son for three long days. How are they feeling during these days? What are they thinking? Finally, on the third day they find him sitting among the teachers in the temple. When Mary and Joseph see him, they are astonished. Mary says to him, "Son, why have you done this to us? Your father and I have been looking for you with great anxiety."

Picture this scene in your mind: a mother and father looking for their lost son for days. What do they say to one another when they meet? What does Mary do when she finds Jesus? What does Joseph do? What does Jesus do?

While the image is fresh in your mind, sit up, open your eyes and go to your reflection booklet. Draw a picture of anything you saw or heard during the reflection.

Engage in Discussion

• There are reasons why parents tell their children to stay with them, or why parents want their children to tell where they are going. Why do you think parents do this?

• Sometimes we may not think a rule is important. When this happens, we need to figure out the reason why the rule was made. What would be a rule you have trouble understanding? Why do you think the rule exists?

• What are appropriate ways to have rules changed?

• How can we follow the rules of our classroom, church, and households, as Jesus tried to follow the rules of his parents, but also of his faith?

Action Step

Each time someone asks you to follow a rule today, stop and think about the reason behind the rule.

Tips for Teaching this Skill

Superstitions and rules that govern life are not the same thing. Is it right for an adult to believe that if you step on a toad you will incur illness or disease? Students in grades three to eight are beginning to think about the difference between rules and superstitions.

The word "rule" comes from the Latin *regere*, "to lead straight." Rules are defined as a prescribed guide for conduct or action, or a standard of judgment. The word "procedure" comes from the Latin *procedere*, "to go forward." Procedures refer to an established way of doing things. The root word for "skills" means "to make a difference." A skill is a learned power of doing a thing competently.

Understanding rules and the reasons for rules is a constructive self-discipline skill, meaning it will be difficult for children in kindergarten through sixth grade to demonstrate on their own without prompting. To practice this skill a person would be able to recognize chaos and perceive a need for order.

When we understand the reasons for rules we wait to make sure a rule is in place. We think: Do I know the reason for this rule? Who can I ask if I do not understand why the rule is in place?

The fewer the rules the better. It is better to have a few rules that everyone knows, and different procedures or ways to follow the rules. Teach children that the procedures may change depending upon the teacher, the subject, their grade level, but the rules will always stay the same.

The criteria for an effective rule is:

- it is stated in the positive;
- it is reasonable;
- it is enforceable;
- it protects the rights of others;
- it has a specific purpose; if it no longer achieves the purpose, it can be changed.

Remember that skills are not the same as rules. You cannot break a skill. You can only learn to do it better!

How It Works

Mrs. Martin is a wonderful teacher! She has a strong reputation for being able to help all her children learn. Mrs. Martin was immediately drawn to the idea of teaching fifteen self-discipline skills because she believed her youngsters would need these skills for the rest of their lives. However, when she started to teach them about understanding rules, she did not expect her thirty-two fifth graders to be so vocal about the existing school procedures. Before the discussion was finished, they were quite upset, voicing their major complaint about the school schedule and not having enough time for Physical Education class more than once a week.

At first Mrs. Martin thought her lesson was a disaster, and that she had opened a can of worms better left untouched. In discussing the issue with peers, she realized how she could use the children's perceptions as an opportunity to allow them to practice the skill of understanding rules. After all, this was the children's issue and not hers. They should be doing the work of trying to figure out how to resolve it.

Once she changed the way she thought about the issue, her attitude and actions also changed. She enthusiastically informed the principal that her students would be doing some research and encouraged the principal to be as supportive as she could because they were practicing a difficult self-discipline skill. Then she spoke to the class. She told them that, in wanting P.E. more than once a week, they obviously noticed a need. She complimented

---

Skill Vocabulary

Use these phrases in class throughout the year to help reinforce understanding of the reasons for rules:

- What is the rule?

- Why do we have that rule?

- Are you willing to work to suggest changes?

- When a procedure becomes so important that everyone should follow it, it becomes a rule.

- Skills are not rules. When rules are not followed there is always a consequence. When a skill is missing, you get another chance to practice the skill.

- Will you use a self-imposed consequence or do you want an adult-imposed consequence?

them on their desire to do something about it. She asked for a group of volunteers who would like to research the issue and come up with suggestions for making changes.

The initial group of sixteen willing participants was soon reduced to a group of five when they were told what their obligations would be. During the first twenty-minute meeting, Mrs. Martin gave them a copy of the state requirements for the number of hours students must be in each class during a school year. They were also given a copy of the P.E. teacher's schedule and the schedule for the current classes. These items were new pieces of information the students had not previously considered.

Mrs. Martin asked one of them to write a letter of introduction which she would sign that would allow them to interview teachers and have access to some matters of public record that they might want to obtain from the school office. The young people were eager to begin and decided they would all write the letter of introduction.

During a brainstorming session they listed all the things they might need to do. They got out their calendars and scheduled meeting times. They scheduled times when they could report back their progress to the class. Someone was assigned to get poster board to illustrate the current schedule. Others were to talk with teachers to see if their classes also wanted more P.E.

Since their work began in January, they set the end of February as their goal for completing this

task. The first week, enthusiasm ran high. On Friday, at the class meeting, the students had designed large posters showing how the schedule currently looked. They told the class they also had spoken with the principal and she encouraged them to do this project. The second week, they reported there were more things to take into consideration than they first thought and it might take a little longer than the end of February to get things worked out.

The third week, the students did not have a chance to meet as a group so there was nothing to report at the class meeting. For the fourth week they reported they were still working on the project but it was harder than they thought. In the fifth week they reported that, while their idea appeared to be a good one, with over 700 children in the school the current schedule was the only one that seemed feasible.

Mrs. Martin complimented the group for trying to resolve the issue. She asked them what they had learned about understanding the reasons for rules. No one complained about the lack of P.E. for the remainder of the year.

Activities

Procedures Checklist

Use this checklist as a guide to procedures for your students to follow throughout the year.

1. Seating arrangement
___Open seating
___Assigned seating
2. Behavior for entering class
___Place belongings in desk, locker, or bookshelf
___Place class materials on desk.
___Copy class work from the board
___Copy homework assignments from the board
Other_____

_____
3. Behavior when leaving the class
___Leave when the bell is sounded
___Leave only when dismissed by the teacher.
4. How to request permission to get drinks, use restroom, etc.
5. Procedure for going to nurse, specialist, office, other classes

Our Perception of Rules
Makes Them
Obstacles or
Opportunities

Revise   Define

Test   RULES   Write

Post   Discuss

6. Homework procedures

7. Procedure for sharpening pencils and requesting supplies

8. What to do when tardy to class

9. Procedure for going to the locker

10. Materials needed for class

11. Procedure if you do not have class materials.

12. Where to put trash

13. Is gum chewing or snacks allowed?

14. How to ask for teacher's assistance

15. When is focused listening needed? What is expected when people listen?

16. Procedure for asking appropriate questions

17. Format for heading papers

18. Procedure for turning in completed work

19. Class policy for make up work

20. Testing schedule

21. Grading policy

22. Structure of class

___Written work

___Small group work

___Independent work

___Large group discussions

___Small group discussions

___Video/media presentations

Other_____

How Do Rules Affect Others?

Teach children that rules can have positive, negative, and interesting effects on others. Invite youngsters to brainstorm about the following situations.

- List five positive, five negative, and five interesting outcomes if there was a rule that all the autos in America had to be blue in color.

- List five positive, five negative, and five interesting outcomes if you woke up one morning and found your entire house had been computerized.

- List five positive, five negative, and five interesting outcomes if everyone followed the advice to feed the hungry and clothe the naked and visit the sick.

Allow time to share ideas and to discuss these three issues. Then help children understand the reasons for rules by discussing the positive, negative, and interesting outcomes that occur because of the rules that exist in your classroom or family.

Rule Charts

Develop a chart, like the one that follows, to describe the rules for your classroom, and how someone who obeys these rules will/will not act. Post your chart and use it throughout the year to review classroom procedures and revise as needed. Remind yourself of all the procedures children need to learn for each teacher.

Classroom Rules

Rule #1 Respect Yourself, Others, and Things

Someone who respects themselves and others

- Is neat and clean in appearance.
- Participates at church services and during prayer.
- Honors other's space and things.
- Is respectful of other's feelings.

Someone who doesn't respect themselves and others

- Is unclean or sloppy in appearance.
- Disturbs others at Mass or prayer.
- Gets into lockers or desks of other children.
- Uses putdowns and gossip.

Rule #2 Contribute to the Learning Environment

Someone who contributes to the learning environment

- Participates and completes assignments.
- Attends class on time.
- Brings materials to class.

Someone who distracts from the learning environment

- Is unwilling to cooperate with others.
- Is tardy or absent.
- Fails to return materials.

Rule #3 Follow School and Classroom Procedures

Someone who follows classroom procedures

- Follows fire and tornado drills.
- Conforms to dress code.

Someone who doesn't follow these procedures

- Uses a phone without permission.
- Brings toys or inappropriate objects to class.
- Chews gum or eats during class.

Handbook Study of School Rules

Divide the class into small groups. Give each group a copy of the school handbook and a list of the questions that follow below. Give them fifteen minutes to:

- Read through the rules in the handbook.
- Suggest a rule the group would like to discuss.
- Discuss the rule and answer the questions on the worksheet.
- Assign a spokesperson who will report what was discussed to the class.

Here is a sample list of questions:

1. What is the reason given in the handbook for the rule?

2. What reason would your group give for the rule?

3. Rate the rule 1-5 1=Great, 2= Good, 3=Fair, 4=Poor 5=Bad

4. Why did your group give it that rating?

5. What happens when the rule is not followed?

6. What do you see happen in practice?

7. What is the consequence for not following the rule?

8. Make a suggestion how this rule or the consequence might be changed to better serve the people in this school.

Create Safety Rules

When children teach rules to others, they are given an opportunity to demonstrate how well or poorly they understand the reason for rules. Introduce junior high and high school youngsters to the task of formulating a rule and designing a strategy to teach younger children about safety rules (fire, drug, environmental, food, water safety).

Ask teens to think of a time safety rules are needed, for example, when riding a bus. What is the safety rule younger children should learn? When waiting for the bus, stand a safe distance from where the bus stops. A good safety rule is to have  the first person in line stand five giant steps away.

Then ask them to think of a method for teaching the rule, i.e., a teaching tool. For example, they could draw five giant steps and cut them out. Give the steps to a child and ask them to place them on the floor. The teen can pretend to be the bus while the child must locate a safe spot—five giant steps away—to wait for the bus.

Another time when you need a safety rule would be when flying a kite. What is the safety rule children should learn? Never fly your kite near electric wires or transmission towers.

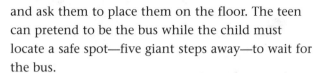

Discuss what the method or teaching tool you can use use to teach the rule. For example, you could teach children this rap to learn about kite safety.

If a kite you like to fly.
Do be safe whenever you try.
Electric wires or transmission towers
Have lots of current and deadly power.
So play it safe whenever you play.
From all electricity keep kites away.

Teach the teens that younger children learn best

- When things are spelled out step-by-step.
- When abstract ideas are made concrete.
- When an older student tells them things about life that they may not yet know.
- When ideas are put into rhymes, riddles, raps, songs, posters, puppets or teaching tools, gestures and body movements.

Invite the teens to write up a brief contract for the grade they would like to receive on the above assignment about teaching school rules to younger children.

To receive an A: Do the assignment completely and neatly, share with the class, volunteer to go to a primary grade and teach the rule using the method I created.

Three rules that all catechists and teachers can adopt are:

1. Respect yourself, others and things.

2. Contribute to the learning environment.

3. Follow class and school procedures.

These three rules can apply in class and in common areas as well as in the home.

To receive a B: Do the assignment completely and neatly and share with the class.

To receive a C: Do the assignment completely, neatly and hand it in without sharing with the class.

Create Rules for Games

Select an ordinary game board and game pieces that children have used before. Invite them to create a new game by rewriting the rules. Test the new written rules and make changes so the game can be fun for everyone involved. Once the rules of the new game have been perfected, invite children to give the game to others to play and critique.

Create Rhyme Mobiles

Primary grade children grasp rules better when they are put into rhyme. Below you will find a sample of rhymes that fourth graders developed for the first grade children. Each fourth grader then designed a 5" x 11" card illustrating the rhyme. Wire hangers and string were used to create a mobile. Here are some examples of rhymes:

- If you share, you will show how to care.

- If you fight, you better be ready to write.

- When you eat, you must take your seat.

- If you are kind, you will be easy to find.

- To show you care, you must share.

- If it is sloppy, you must recopy!

- If you hit, you must sit.

- If my eyes you cannot see, don't begin to speak to me.

Use Children's Literature

Mick Harte Was Here, Barbara Park. In this story about siblings, family, and bicycle safety, Phoebe tells of her younger brother Mick in a bicycle accident, which might not have been fatal had he been wearing his helmet.

Miss Nelson Is Missing! Harry Allard. Miss Nelson was getting exasperated with her class. What was she going to do? One day she disappears, and her substitute, Viola Swamp, takes over this mischievous class. Will they be stuck with Viola Swamp forever?

Stop, Drop, and Roll, Margery Cuyler. Jessica is worried about fire safety, and worries that she won't be able to remember "Stop, Drop, and Roll!" when asked to demonstrate the procedure for her school. Readers will pick up important safety tips.

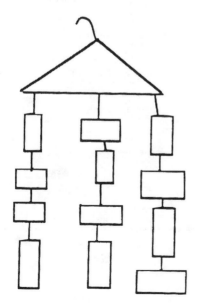

RIGHTS AND RESPONSIBILITIES

Intermediate grade students learn about rules by talking about rights and responsibilities. The letter below can be modified and given to youngsters at the beginning of the year to teach them about rules and the reasons for rules.

Dear Students,

Welcome to a new year of learning! In addition to all the different subjects you will learn about this year, you will also be given a chance to learn about yourself. You have a right to know this information. With every right comes a responsibility. Do you know some of your rights as a student? Do you know the responsibilities that go along with these rights? Some of your rights and responsibilities include:

Right
1. To learn about myself.
2. To be safe in religion class/school and to expect my property to be safe.
3. To hear and be heard. This means no one will yell, scream, or disturb my learning.
4. To be helped to learn self-control. No one will silently stand by while I abuse the rights of others or when others abuse my rights.
5. To expect that these rights will be mine in all circumstances as long as I am doing my responsibility.

Responsibility
1. To contribute to the learning environment so others can learn.
2. Not to steal or destroy the property of others.
3. Help keep a calm and quiet learning area. I will not yell, make loud noises, scream or disturb others.
4. To learn self-control. I will expect to be corrected when I abuse the rights of others. I will accept the criticism in a respectful manner.
5. To protect my right and the rights of others by exercising my responsibilities in all circumstances.
For your first homework assignment show this list of rights and responsibilities to a parent and bring back revisions or additions.

Your teacher,

CHAPTER 8

Accomplishing Tasks

Then he put him on his own animal, brought him to an inn, and took care of him. (Luke 10:34)

Reflection: How do I help my students work with the gifts God has given them?

These are the steps to accomplishing a task

1. Brainstorm at last three different ways to accomplish the same task.

2. Select the way that will best help you accomplish your goal.

3. Set a realistic time limit.

4. Follow your plan.

5. Continue to work on your plan even if you don't finish the job.

6. Evaluate the results.

Someone who accomplishes a task on their own

- Makes a plan.
- Sets a realistic goal.
- Works until finished.
- Finishes on time.
- Negotiates for more time if needed.
- Doesn't waste work time.
- Doesn't work without focus.
- Doesn't leave a task unfinished.
- Doesn't turn work in late.
- Doesn't give up.

GUIDED REFLECTION

As we begin our reflection, prepare to listen to a reading from Scripture. Close your eyes. Take a deep breath and feel your body relax. Feel your feet and legs relax. Notice your arms and head feeling heavy. Your breathing has slowed down.

A scholar asked Jesus, "Teacher, what must I do to have eternal life?" The reply was, "You shall love the Lord with all your heart, mind and strength, and love your neighbor as yourself." The scholar then asked Jesus, "Who is my neighbor?" Jesus replied with this story:

ACCOMPLISH A TASK

"A man was traveling to Jericho. At night he was jumped by a band of robbers. They beat him and left him to die. A priest saw him and passed him by on the opposite side of the street. A Levite came up to him and upon seeing him, passed by on the opposite side. But, a Samaritan traveler who came upon him was moved with compassion at the sight. He approached the victim, poured oil and wine over his wounds, and bandaged them. He lifted him up onto his own animal, took him to an inn, and cared for him.

The next day he gave the innkeeper two silver coins with the instructions, "Take care of him." At this point, Jesus turned to the scholar and asked, "Which of these three was a neighbor to the victim?"

Picture in your mind what each person did when they saw the stranger. Keep this image in your mind as you slowly open your eyes. Now take out your reflection booklet and draw a picture of anything you saw or heard during this reflection.

When most of the children have completed their illustrations, invite them to look at their pictures and describe what they saw or heard.

Engage in Discussion

• What three words could we use to describe the quality of care the Samaritan gave to the stranger?
• Summarize the story by telling the students that the Samaritan was compassionate toward someone whom he didn't know. He not only helped him physically, he also helped him monetarily, without asking for compensation. When he cared for the stranger he did so in a quality way. He did his very best.
• In what practical ways can we help others as the good Samaritan did?

Action Step

Today, whenever you are given a task to do, think about the quality of care you put into doing the task. Try of make it your very best work.

Tips for Teaching this Skill

When a Native American girl comes of age in some tribes, she signifies this passage by weaving a unique design into a basket. Each one is different.

Figuring out on your own how to accomplish a task is a constructive self-discipline skill, meaning it will be difficult for children in kindergarten through sixth grade to demonstrate on their own without prompting. This skill is more complex than simply following instructions. Now the person must come up with their own plan to complete the task.

Younger children can learn to accomplish tasks by following the system others put into place. Older students demonstrate this skill when they begin to figure out how to do something on their own.

When we figure out how to accomplish a task we wait until we have learned the boundaries or rules for finishing the task. We think: do I know how to do the job? What plan of action can I take to get this job done? Can I do the entire job or just a portion of it?

Primary grade children will develop the foundation for doing this skill as they follow the procedures and systems put in place by adults who are competent and organized. They begin to demonstrate the skill when they are given socially approved choices and must select one over another.

Primary grade children are helped to do this skill when adults verbalize why different procedures apply in different situations. "Today, because we are in a circle formation rather than in rows, you do not have to raise your hand when you want to speak. Listen and watch and share the conversation when you have something to say."

Intermediate grade children learn how to do this skill by distinguishing between routines and no routines. Youngsters can discover how they work best and how they prefer to work even if it is different from everyone else.

When you use this skill in the classroom, tell the children what portion of the assignment or task they must do as you have directed, and what portion they are free to do differently. Use language such as this: "These are the givens." "This is where you can practice the skill of figuring out on your own how to do the task."

When children practice the important self-discipline skill of learning how to accomplish tasks, adults should act as guides or resource persons who enable and encourage the child's progress. Before giving a child a task to accomplish, three questions can be asked to determine the degree of control or ownership the child would like to have in completing the task:

1. Will you do this job as well as or better than I can?

2. What is your plan for completing this job?

3. Would you like the entire job or only a portion of it?

When routinely asked, these questions can help a child critically think about the goal or outcome of the project.

How It Works

A group of junior high teachers were eating their lunch at a cafeteria table. Around them, almost a hundred junior high students were also eating.

Jamie, an eighth grader, came up to the teachers' table and hovered behind her favorite English teacher, Miss North. "Miss North, Miss North," said

---

Skill Vocabulary

Use these phrases in class throughout the year to help reinforce the skill of accomplishing a task:

• This is all I can tell you. Now you must decide for yourself. Be creative.

• There are many ways to do things. Who can describe one way? Is this your best work? What grade would you give yourself?

• I have a challenge for you.

• Have you considered this as an option?

• Your ideas are original. How can you package the finished product to make it more appealing?

• If I turn this task over to you, will you do the job as well as I can or better?

• Do you have a plan? Do you want the entire job or just a portion of it?

• I'd like to tell you how your performance matched my expectation.

• What if half of your friends did this and half of your friends did that—what would you do?

Jamie, "are you having a good lunch?" "Yes, Jamie," said Miss. North, somewhat perturbed. "I've got to talk to you," said Jamie. "Not now," said Miss. North. "Can't you see I'm eating my lunch?"

Jamie went away, but thirty seconds later she was back. Again she tried to get Miss North to notice her. This time, Miss North sounded a little more angry. "I'll talk with you when I am finished." A third time Jamie decided to return to get Miss North's attention. When the teacher saw her coming, she moved her chair away from the table and pretended she was going to get up and chase after Jamie. Jamie ran away.

Miss North turned to the teachers at the table and said, "She always does this to me." "Do you mind if I talk to her?" asked Mrs. Flynn. "Go ahead," said Miss North.

As Jamie was making her way back to the teacher's table for the fourth time, Mrs. Flynn got up and met her before she got half way there. "Jamie," said Mrs. Flynn. "I noticed that you really need to speak to Miss North, but this is not the right time or way to get her attention."

"She always does this to me," said Jamie. "Maybe she does," said Mrs. Flynn, "but Miss North has a right to eat her lunch in peace, and right now you are disturbing that right. I want you to move away from the table and think about another way you might be able to get her attention that would be agreeable to her. Can I have your cooperation in this matter?"

"Yes, Mrs. Flynn," said Jamie.

Later that afternoon Miss North came to Mrs. Flynn and asked, "What did you say to Jamie?" "Why?" asked Mrs. Flynn.

"Because she came up to me after lunch," said Miss North, "and asked if she could make an appointment to talk to me. We just talked for twenty minutes and it was the best conversation we have ever had."

Mrs. Flynn told Miss North there was no secret in what she did. "I just recognized that she did not know how to get your attention in the proper way and told her she had to figure out on her own another way to accomplish this task. I guess she did it!"

Activities

Practice Being Observant

Ask for two volunteers to practice the skill. You will need two different family magazines or sections of the Sunday newspaper. The task is simple.

Each person will be given a certain number of minutes to clip all the saving coupons from his or her magazine or newspaper. The goals are to figure out a way to do this job in the time allotted and to do it thoroughly so that not one coupon is left in the magazine or paper.

At the end of the time period, exchange magazines and invite each volunteer to discover how thoroughly the other person completed the task. Discuss together:

- the method or way the person accomplished the task;
- hints or pointers they would give to someone else doing the job for the first time;
- a plan for using the coupons that have been clipped.

Different Ways to Do the Same Job

Have fun exploring the fact that one job can be accomplished in many different ways. Select a favorite comic strip that has several frames to it, or a picture with a humorous caption. Cut off the dialogue or caption. Glue the strip to paper, and make copies so each person can participate in this activity.

Set a time limit of ten minutes. Let persons work individually or in teams to create a new dialogue that would go with the pictures. Share the finished products. Talk about how people have different ideas about similar things. Explore other times in school or at home when something can have different meanings to different people. Discuss ways to handle these differences.

Examine Textbooks

Give intermediate grade students time to investigate their various textbooks they will use during a school year. Invite them to find ten features of any one book they like. After the period of investigation, invite them to act as salespersons and sell the book to the class. This same activity can be done using library books.

Delegating Tasks

When we give the children a task to complete, we delegate that task to them. To delegate means to empower another to act on our behalf.

The following form can be duplicated and given to children in grades four and up whenever they are taking responsibility for tasks. An adult would complete sections A, B, C, D, and F. Discuss the form after the child(ren) has completed section E.

A. Delegated job:

_____

B. Person delegating the job:

_____

C. Person who will complete the task:

_____

D. Job needed by (date):

_____

E. I believe I can do this job as well as or better than another person. This is my plan:

Step #1

_____

Step #2

_____

Step #3

_____

Step #4

_____

Step #5

_____

I understand the task you are giving to me, and my responsibilities in completing it. I also understand the items checked below. Yes_____ No_____

F. I will:

_____Take full control of this job. Do it without any further contact with the teacher.

_____Take action, but let the teacher know what I'm doing and when I finish.

_____Find a partner and look into this problem, if necessary.

_____Come up with some solutions to the problem and then come and discuss my plans with my teacher before taking action.

_____Think about this job and make a list of the actions I think should be taken and those that should not be taken. I will listen to the recommendations of my teacher in making a decision about a plan of action.

Create Big Books

Children in intermediate grades enjoy creating their own books. Students can work in groups to create books about the fifteen self-discipline skills, holidays, events from history, traditional celebrations or fiction stories.

Make a sample big book to show the students the components that must be present in their finished product. Punch three holes in the pages and insert metal rings to hold the finished book together. Using the guidelines given below, the youngsters must come up with a plan to accomplish the task on their own.

Take eight sheets of 11" x 17" card stock. Write one of the following guidelines on each sheet.

- Easy for young people to read.
- Drawings that are clear and simple.
- Something to be preserved and placed in the media center.
- Created by people who practice cooperation.
- Each group will need an idea person, organizer, illustrator, and writer.
- Created by people who have to figure out how to accomplish a task.
- Steps needed:
  1. Decide on a plan.
  2. Decide on the number of pages in your book.
  3. Get materials.
  4. Assign tasks.
  5. Begin creating.

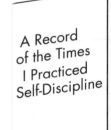

Hang these on a bulletin board or around the classroom so the children can easily refer to them as they are creating their books.

Self-Evaluation Booklet

When youngsters are just learning the constructive skills, they benefit from having some way to organize the information they are learning and the skill practices they engage in. Give each child twenty blank 5" x 8" index cards or 8 1/2" x 11" card stock.

- Two cards would be used as a front and back covers.
- Fifteen would be used for the fifteen skills.

- One would be used as an introduction page listing the name, age, hobbies, and a short biography of the person who will be using the book.

- One would be used as a summary page at the end of the book.

- Bind the cards together using metal rings, string, or a standard binding comb.

Invite the children to decorate and personalize the front and back covers of their booklets. Inform students that they will be expected to turn in the booklet at the end of the school year. It will be their record of the opportunities they have had to practice each of the skills. They can record times at school, at home, with friends, on trips, etc., when they consciously chose to use a self-discipline skill. They may write on and illustrate each page.

Throughout the year, select one self-discipline skill per week for the students to work on. Discuss with them what is already known about the skill. Make a list of tips on how best to demonstrate the skill. Use the following questions as a guide:

- What should people know about this skill?

- How does a person practice this skill so it benefits other people?

- Why do you want to practice this skill?

- What do you plan to do?

Encourage the students to add to the booklet over the school year. Poetry, stories, songs, and pictures that highlight a skill can be put on the back of each card. Keep your camera handy to that you can take pictures of the students as they practice their skills, and give them copies of the photos for their book.

This book can become the student's self-discipline portfolio for the school year.

Review the Right Way/Wrong Way

Whenever children role play, they are given an opportunity to figure out on their own how to accomplish a task. Intermediate grade and junior high students are particularly interested in this type of activity.

To try this with your students, prepare twenty or more category cards to introduce this review. The children can then be challenged to create their own situations. Working in teams of three, the children select a card. They are given one day to meet with their team and prepare a role play that would show

the wrong way to accomplish something, and the right way to use self-discipline skills to accomplish this. A sample of the situations that might appear on the cards could include

- The right way/wrong way to resolve a problem

- The right way/wrong way to use social skills

- The right way/wrong way to separate fact from feeling

- The right way/wrong way to enter the classroom

- The right way/wrong way to end your day at school

- The right way/wrong way to get the teacher's attention

- The right way/wrong way to ask permission

- The right way/wrong way to pray

- The right way/wrong way to behave in church

Use Children's Literature

A Picture Book of George Washington Carver, David Adler. This is a simple but informative biography of the African-American scientist who overcame tremendous hardship to make unusual and important discoveries in the field of agriculture.

Saint Joan of Arc: God's Soldier, Susan Helen Wallace. Young Joan is called by God to see that the rightful heir is crowned king. To do so she has to make the ultimate sacrifice.

Helen Keller: Courage in the Dark, Johanna Hurwitz. A biography of the blind and deaf girl who overcame both handicaps with the help of her teacher, Annie Sullivan.

Salt in His Shoes: Michael Jordan in Pursuit of a Dream, Deloris Jordan. Michael Jordan's mother and sister share a story from his childhood. He worries about his small size when playing basketball with his older brothers. His mother advises him to put salt in his shoes and say a prayer every night. His father tells him that practice and determination, not height, are what he needs.

CHAPTER 9

Exhibiting Leadership

Then Moses stretched out his hand over the sea…and the Israelites went into the sea on dry ground. (Exodus 14:21–22)

Reflection: How can children show their leadership by doing God's will even when it isn't cool?

A leader is a person who

1. Sees the needs of others and considers them important.

2. Stands on the side of truth, even if they stand alone.

3. Acts on behalf of another, even if he or she is inconvenienced.

Someone who is a leader

- Thinks about other people.
- Acts for the good of others.
- Stands up for what is right.
- Talks to everyone and doesn't exclude others.
- Can be trusted.
- Doesn't ignore others' needs.
- Doesn't go along with something when it's not right.
- Doesn't give up when it's hard to help others.

GUIDED REFLECTION

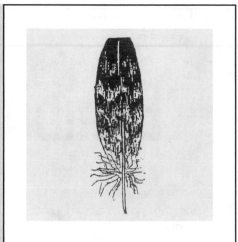

LEADERSHIP

As we begin our reflection, prepare to listen to a reading from Scripture. Close your eyes. Take a deep breath and feel your body relax. Feel your feet and legs relax. Notice your arms and head are feeling heavy. Your breathing has slowed down.

Go back in time and picture the earth long before Jesus was born. Try to picture the time in which Moses lived in Egypt. There would be pyramids and desert lands. Moses was an old man who had listened to God most of his life. God told Moses he would help him lead the Israelites out of Egypt, where they were in slavery, into the desert where they would be free. Many, many people were walking out of Egypt being led by Moses. But the Pharaoh and his soldiers did not want them to go, so they mounted their horses and marched out into the desert after the Israelites. As they came closer and closer, the Israelites grew afraid. Moses stayed calm and said, "Fear not! The Lord will have a victory for you today."

When it was dark, Moses stretched out his hand over the sea. The Lord swept the sea with a strong east wind and turned it into dry land. When the water was divided, the Israelites marched into the midst of the sea following Moses, with the water like a wall to their right and to their left.

Pharaoh's soldiers marched into the sea after them. But as soon as the Israelites were safe with Moses on the other side, the wall of water collapsed, sweeping away Pharaoh's people. Moses, with God's help, saved the Israelites.

Picture in your mind what Moses did for the Israelites. Keep this image in your mind as you slowly open your eyes. Now take out your reflection booklet and draw a picture of anything you saw or heard during this reflection.

When most of the children have completed their illustrations, invite them to look at their pictures and describe what they saw or heard.

Engage in Discussion

• Moses was a strong leader. He had faith that God would help him and his followers find safety. He was a leader who saw and considered the needs of others, stood on the side of truth even if he stood alone, and acted on behalf of another even if it was difficult to do so.

• Ask students how Moses' actions showed these qualities. How can we show these qualities, as well as Moses' leadership skills?

• How can we develop the courage to go where our faith leads us?

Action Step

Look for opportunities to be a leader like Moses during the coming week.

Tips for Teaching this Skill

The eagle was able to fly the highest and take concerns and prayers to the heavens. That's why for Native Americans, the eagle feather is a sign of leadership.

Leadership is a constructive self-discipline skill, meaning it will be difficult for children in kindergarten through sixth grade to demonstrate on their own without prompting. Whenever someone takes on a leadership position from another, they are given power to get the job done. Sometimes this power is delegated to another by someone in authority.

When we practice being a leader, we wait until we have observed the needs of others. We think: what course of action will make life better for people? Do I think this person's needs are important? Am I willing to act even if I am the only one? Am I willing to be inconvenienced for the sake of another?

The more opportunities children have to practice the skill of leadership, the better equipped they will be to assume leadership positions when they are older. No matter what age a person is, leadership can be practiced if it can be translated into concrete actions or activities.

Children have a right to know the values of their heroes and leaders. There are hidden qualities about these people that are not always obvious to children. They echo the three qualities of leadership listed in the beginning of this chapter. A hero/leader:

- Sees the needs of others and consider them to be important.
- Stands on the side of truth even if they stand alone.
- Acts on behalf of others even if they are inconvenienced.

How It Works

Mrs. Beth Augustine decided to introduce her fifth graders to the three qualities of a leader at the beginning of the school year. Each week she asked the youngsters to decide to practice being a leader. They reviewed what a leader would look like and sound like, and this is what they decided:

A leader was someone who saw the needs of others and thought they were important; stood on the side of truth even if they stood alone; and was willing to be inconvenienced for the sake of others.

During one of the first weeks of practicing the leadership skill, the fifth grade boys were ready to leave the lunch table with papers and debris left under and on top of the table. Rather than just tell them to pick up the mess before they left, Mrs. Augustine asked, "Please raise your hand if you are looking for opportunities to practice leadership today?" About seven hands went up.

Then she asked, "Who would be willing to practice it now and clean up the mess at the lunch table?" All the hands went down, except for one. "I'll do it," said Jeremy. Mrs. Augustine thanked him and started up the steps with the rest of the class.

On the way to the classroom two of Jeremy's classmates made the comment. "Jeremy really is a leader, Mrs. Augustine."

"Why do you say that?" the teacher asked.

"Because he was the only one willing to inconvenience himself to help."

Mrs. Augustine said later that she knew the boys in the class had reached a new level of understanding how leadership could be practiced.

Leaders Have Class

Form an acronym using the fifteen self-discipline skills. For example:

Cooperates
Listens
Asks questions when something is not understood
Selects proper procedures to accomplish a task.
Socially interacts well with others

Skill Vocabulary

Use these phrases in class throughout the year to help reinforce leadership skills:

- A leader is someone willing to stand on the side of truth even if they stand alone.
- A leader is someone willing to be inconvenienced for the sake of others.
- A leader notices when someone is in need and makes a decision to offer to help.
- What would a leader look like and/or sound like in this situation?

Activities

Lead Yourself

Good leaders start by learning to lead themselves. They know what they can do well and what they need help with.

The purpose of this activity will be to see who knows themselves the best. To begin, divide the students into groups of four or more. Give everyone a 3" x 5" card and tell them to write their name on the top of the card. There are three categories for the groups to talk about: talents and gifts; special skills and interests; and things I need help with.

Begin the session by sharing one item about yourself. Next, choose two people from one of the groups and ask if they agree with your statement. If you receive agreement from both persons, list the item on your card. If either or both do not agree, that person must tell how their perception differs from your statement.

Now direct the groups to continue this process, moving from person to person within the group. The first person to list three items will be the winner. If time runs out before the game is over, negotiate to continue at a later time.

Special Qualities of Leadership

Leaders exhibit two special qualities.

- They work to build people up.
- They are honest and work for the good of the group or family.

Duplicate copies of the leadership card pictured below. Give each person who wants to practice leadership a copy. Invite them to monitor themselves and observe others for one week. Each time they demonstrate one of the two qualities of a leader,

---

My Leadership Card		
Name _____		
Quality	**Checks**	**Key word**
Worked to build people up		
Worked for the good of a group by being honest		

---

they should place a check mark on the card. Next to the leadership quality they can write a key word to help them remember what they did.

At the end of a week, invite everyone to report their progress. Set personal goals to try and improve leadership skills and repeat the process for another week. Continue the activity until the group decides it is time to work on another self-discipline skill.

Test School Leaders

Test students to see who might be capable of representing the school in leadership positions. Some or all of these items might be on the test.

- Give an example of acceptable and unacceptable behavior for membership in the parish or school community.
- Discuss the difference between discipline and self-discipline.
- Explain how everyone is responsible for their behavior and give examples.
- List and explain the rules of the faith formation program or school.
- State the address and phone number of the religious education office or school.
- Explain the mission and motto of the religious education program or school, if these criteria are applicable to your situation.

Guidelines for Practicing Leadership

Ten high school students from Omaha, Nebraska developed a list of qualities they believe leaders exhibit. Share the list of qualities with your students and invite them to add items.

- Do whatever it takes to accomplish a task, even if it takes more work and less play.
- Have a larger social circle and aren't afraid to make new friends.
- Shine when they lead, but are also open to new ideas.
- Should be able to speak their minds clearly so others can understand them.
- Respect everyone's ideas.
- Restrain their impulsivity.
- Teach others to become leaders.
- Stick up for the little guy.
- Are trustworthy in every situation.

CHAPTER 10

Communicating Effectively

"Pray then in this way: Our Father in heaven, hallowed be your name...." (Matthew 6:9)

Reflection: How do I help my students form a prayer life that will allow them to communicate with God?

The skills of good communication are

1. Proper verbal and nonverbal communication.

2. Good listening skills.

3. Respect for different points of view.

4. Avoidance of negative styles of speaking about others.

5. Questions that begin with W or H to discover what is important.

6. Ending on a positive note.

A person who knows how to communicate

• Pays attention to the person talking.

• Uses listening skills.

• Has a positive attitude.

• Confronts others only with the intention of making changes.

• Doesn't ignore the speaker.

• Isn't distracted.

• Doesn't use sarcasm, gossip, or putdowns.

• Doesn't try to manipulate or overpower others.

GUIDED REFLECTION

COMMUNICATION

As we begin our reflection, prepare to listen to a reading from Scripture. Close your eyes. Take a deep breath and feel your body relax. Feel your feet and legs relax. Notice your arms and head feeling heavy. Your breathing has slowed down.

Let your mind journey back to the time of Jesus. Picture Jesus sitting on a rock on the top of a mountain. There are crowds of people all around him. His disciples are with him, too. The people are quiet because they want to hear everything Jesus has to say. He is their teacher. Today, Jesus wants to teach his disciples and anyone who wants to listen, how to pray.

Jesus tells them "When you pray, do not be like those who stand and pray on the street corners so that others may see them. Drawing attention to themselves is their only reward. But when you pray, go to your room, close the door, and pray to your Father in secret. Your Father who sees you pray in secret will repay you. Do not babble like those who think they will be heard because of their many words. Your Father knows what you need before you even ask him."

"Pray then in this way: Our Father in heaven, hallowed be your name. Your kingdom come. Your will be done, on earth as it is in heaven. Give us this day our daily bread. And forgive us our debts, as we also have forgiven our debtors. And do not bring us to the time of trial, but rescue us from the evil one."

Picture in your mind Jesus teaching his disciples about prayer. Keep this image in your mind as you slowly open your eyes. Now take out your reflection booklet and draw a picture of anything you saw or heard during this reflection.

When most of the children have completed their illustrations, invite them to look at their pictures and describe what they saw or heard.

Engage in Discussion

• Jesus was a good teacher and storyteller. What do you think Jesus did to communicate with the people around him?
• What are some ways we can show others that we have positive verbal and nonverbal communication skills?
• How can we develop a habit of prayer so that we can communicate regularly with God?

Action Step

Each time you encounter someone, be a positive communicator. Use some of the communication techniques Jesus used.

Tips for Teaching this Skill

The talking stick is used to record historical moments in the life of a Native American tribe. It becomes the written communication of the life of a people.

Communication is a constructive self-discipline skill, meaning it will be difficult for students in kindergarten through sixth grade to demonstrate on their own without prompting.

When we communicate, we wait until the other person has finished speaking. We think: what words will correctly represent how I think and feel?

To build the foundation for this skill, primary children can be taught:

- how to read facial expressions and body postures to learn if something is liked or disliked by others;
- vocabulary words to build comprehension;
- to think before they speak;
- the difference between helpful and hurtful messages.

Intermediate grade students benefit from established routines which include reporting facts and opinions to the class.

In a group discussion teach this maxim: No person should speak twice before all who wish to speak have spoken once.

How It Works

The Franklins are a wonderful family with seven children. When the oldest son was seventeen years old, he was picked up for having an open bottle of liquor in his car.

It was after midnight when the police called the boy's parents and asked for someone to come and pick him up. The parents were shocked, especially Mr. Franklin, who was very angry and hurt. As he dressed to go the police station, his wife reminded him. "Fred, our son will be scared. Listen to him."

These words must have rumbled around inside Mr. Franklin's head all the way to the police station. When he got there, he found his son very embarrassed. The boy hung his head and stood up against the wall waiting for his father's response. Everything the father had planned to say, left him. In his total vulnerability, he communicated the only way he could. He hugged his boy and they both wept.

Skill Vocabulary

Use these phrases in class throughout the year to help reinforce communication skills:

- I don't believe you have established the tone of voice you will want to take during our discussion. Please try again.
- Your idea is good, but your choice of words is offensive. Please say it over.
- Please use the criteria for a good conversation.
- Are you giving a helpful or hurtful message?
- Tell me a better word (e.g., less offensive, harsh) to use instead of_____.
- You can have the last word on this subject.
- What have you learned that you didn't know before we had this talk?

That night on the journey home, a new relationship was born between father and son. For the first time, it dawned on the boy that his father had loved him unconditionally. For the first time, the father thought of the many lost opportunities he might have had to tell his son how much he loved him.

When the day of his court case arrived, both mother and father stood on either side of their son. The judge issued a sentence of community service with these words, "Son, you have wonderful parents. They love you very much to be here with you."

Activities

Practice Conversation Dialogues

Create a dialogue between two people. Use as many ingredients of the skill of communication as you can. You and your partner can determine who will be involved in the conversation.

Suggestions include: an administrator and a student; you and a saint; you and a teacher; a teacher and a parent; a movie star and a fan; a politician and a voter; and an apostle and Jesus.

Ask for volunteers to role play their conversation in front of the class. Discuss techniques and award points for each element of a good conversation demonstrated by the volunteers.

The Ingredients of a Good Conversation

Teach and then role play a situation that demonstrates the seven ingredients of a good conversation.

1. Demonstrate a willingness to contribute to the conversation. (Includes facial and body posture, as well as depth of response. No one-word answers.)

2. Use good listening skills.

3. Show respect for the other person's point of view.

4. Demonstrate a sense of humor.

5. Avoid sarcasm, hostility, and defensiveness in tone and attitude.

6. Try to understand the other person's world by asking questions that begin with W and H.

7. Emphasize ideas, books, projects, sports as topics of conversation.

Change It!

Share this saying with students. If you don't like something, change it. If you can't change it, change the way you think about it, don't complain!.

Tell the children about a time in your life when you had to change a negative thought pattern. Invite them to brainstorm a list of actions or ideas they currently complain about. Challenge them to work in teams to try to find a new way to look at an old topic. Select one issue a week to work on collectively to improve communication.

Conversation Stoppers

Intermediate grade students were asked to come up with some reasons why people use putdowns, tattling, and gossip as a form of communication. They replied that:

People put others down because

- they get mad;
- they think this is a smart way to let others know they don't care;
- they like this form of humor;
- they are insecure;
- they want to save face;
- they don't know how to solve a problem by talking about it;
- they think it gives them power.

People tattle because

Facts about Putdowns, Tattling, & Complaining

Putdowns

- Reveal insecurity. People put others down because they do not feel comfortable with themselves. They sometimes lack self-confidence.

- Even if people laugh at putdowns, inside they may not like it and may find a way to get even. Often they pay the person back when they least expect it, and the other person feels betrayed.

- Putdowns cause others to think less, not more of you. Kids who are well liked are people who make others feel comfortable and good, not uncomfortable, about themselves.

- Children usually use putdowns at a vulnerable time in their life, when they need to feel good about themselves, not destroy each other's self-esteem.

- When putdowns are used as a type of humor, both parties should feel comfortable with this type of humor.

- People sometimes use put-downs because they are not comfortable with their feelings or do not know how to express themselves.

Tattling & Complaining

- Tattling is appropriate when a person's life or property is in danger.

- Many older students using tattling as a form of communication because they want to get someone else in trouble. Usually this means they do not know how to fix a problem on their own.

- Sometimes people tattle to get attention, hoping someone will notice them.

- Sometimes people tattle so they can seem better than someone else.

- In place of tattling or complaining, talking with others and getting a third part to help resolve problems is a better way to use your self-discipline skills.

- You can always ask yourself this question. Am I tattling to help or hurt someone? Have I done everything I can to help solve the problem?

- they want to get the other person in trouble;
- they are reporting what they see to someone who can do something about it;
- they don't know what else to do;
- they don't know how to confront other people;
- there are inconsistencies in rules or the way rules are followed.

People gossip because

- they don't know what to talk about;
- it makes them feel important because they have "news" to tell that others might not have;
- they can't keep secrets;
- they don't know the seven ingredients of a good conversation.

Discuss these statements with your class. Invite them to work in teams to revise them and to make the list represent the way they think about these forms of communication. Challenge them to monitor their behavior for one week to determine the number of times they engaged in tattling, gossiping, or put-downs as a form of communication.

Many schools designate areas as no-putdown zones. After conducting a discussion on tattling and complaining as well as gossiping as ineffective forms of communication, invite students to create signs for No Tattling Zones, No Complaining Zones, and No Gossip Zones. Challenge them to visit other classes and talk to students telling them why these forms of conversations are unproductive. Direct them to place signs around the school building where they think these activities are most likely to happen.

Use Communication Cards

Using the cards below as a guide, make a set of four signal cards on different color paper. You can also have each student make their own set of cards.

These communication cards can be stored in a central location. Either the teacher or a youngster can elect to use the cards for classroom discussions or when new material is being taught.

In a discussion, ask anyone who wants to add to the conversation to raise the card with the plus sign if they have something positive to say, or the minus sign if they disagree with what is said. Any child who does not want to participate or answer questions can pass by using the wait-a-minute card. Each person can be directed to use each card only once during a group discussion.

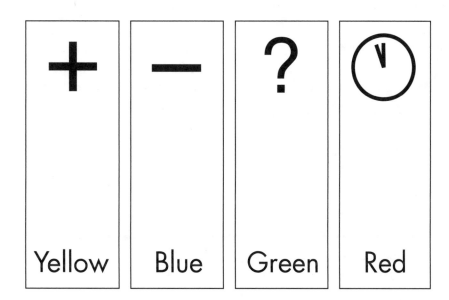

+ = I agree, or have something to add. (yellow)
– = I disagree or see it from another point of view. (blue)
? = I have a question about the topic. (green)
Clock = Wait a minute. I need more time to think. (red)

Class or Family Meetings

Practice effective communication by inviting your class or members of your family to dialogue about issues of importance to one another. Follow this procedure.

- Set a specific time for the meeting. Ten to fifteen minutes is usually ideal.
- Direct members of the group to sit in a circle.
- Place a candle in the center of the circle and use it as the focal point for people who wish to speak (see below).
- Go over the rules for meetings. Here are a few that you can start with, then add guidelines that make sense for your own group.

1. Everyone in the group will have a chance to speak before anyone speaks a second time.

2. Members of the group should use good listening skills.

3. Nonverbal communication or gesturing is not allowed.

Try this technique at your next meeting, if logistics allow. Ask each person who wants to contribute something to the conversation to take the candle and place it in front of them. When they are finished giving their opinion or ideas, they can place the candle back in the center of the circle.

To help keep the conversation focused and flowing, develop a series of questions that can be posted on a flip chart or poster. Here are a few starters:

- What are you most looking forward to this week?
- What one activity do you wish were over? Why?
- How can a member of this group help you this week?
- What is one self-discipline skill you will practice this week?
- Which self-discipline skill do you demonstrate the most? The least?
- What would you like the group to pray for?

Ask members of the group to add other questions that are of interest or concern to them.

A Story about Leadership and Communication

Corky was twelve when he stood up to a group of his friends. He refused to skateboard down a hilly road and tried to talk the others into doing the same because no one was wearing a helmet. He was teased and called names by his buddies. Finally, unable to convince his friends not to skateboard down the hill, he went home.

Later that evening his mother asked why he was so quiet. Reluctantly, Corky told her what had happened. His mother was tempted to comfort him and compliment him for being an obedient son, but she realized that what he had done was much more than that. On his own, without any adult around he had listened to his "best self" and chose to do what he thought was right, even though his friends had used putdowns and teasing in response.

So his mother said, "Corky, it appears to me that you acted like a leader today."

"What do you mean, Mom?" replied Corky.

"Well, you stood on the side of truth even though you stood alone. That's one of the the skills demonstrated by a leader. You also did not give in to using putdowns in responding to the others."

"You're right, Mom," said Corky. "Even though the other kids chose not to listen, I was able to stand up for what I thought was right. It bothered me that they were rude to me, but I know I did the right thing. Maybe I need to think about whether these kids are really my friends."

Corky's mother knew that she had conveyed an important message to her son. She saw that even though there sometimes was a price to pay, he was practicing his self-discipline skills in a focused and direct manner.

74

CHAPTER 11

Organizing Time, Space, People, and Things

You also must be ready, for the Son of Man is coming at an unexpected hour. (Luke 12:40)

Reflection: How do I teach my students stewardship of their time, space and things?

We can learn to organize

1. *Time*. Be aware of time schedules and value them. Plan ahead and follow through. Evaluate the success of time management.

2. *Space*. Keep the environment orderly.

3. *People*. Know procedures to conduct orderly meetings and gatherings.

4. *Things*. Recognize opportunities to simplify and organize material things.

Someone who can organize

- Decides what they need to do.
- Makes lists and prioritizes time.
- Organizes materials.
- Delegates tasks.
- Doesn't work without goals or a plan.
- Doesn't live with clutter.
- Doesn't think they can do it all themselves.

GUIDED REFLECTION

ORGANIZATION

As we begin our reflection, prepare to listen to a reading from Scripture. Close your eyes. Take a deep breath and feel your body relax. Feel your feet and legs relax. Notice your arms and head feeling heavy. Your breathing has slowed down.

Once again, we will begin by picturing Jesus surrounded by a crowd of people. See the crippled, distressed faces of the people in the crowd. Some have open wounds or ulcers. Others just want to be near Jesus to learn from him. The people closest to Jesus were his apostles.

Jesus asked them this question: "If the master of the house had known the hour when a thief was coming, would he let his house be broken into?" "No," said the disciples very convincingly. "Well, then, you must also be prepared," said Jesus, "for at an hour you do not expect, the Son of Man will come." Jesus wanted his disciples to try to live like a person who loved God and show that love by loving others, even their enemies.

If you were sitting at the feet of Jesus listening to his words, what would you like Jesus to know about how you spend your time? Why do you think it would be important to tell him about how you love God? Picture yourself talking to Jesus. Tell him the three things that are most important to you in your life right now.

Keep this image in your mind as you slowly open your eyes. Now take out your reflection booklet and draw a picture of anything you saw or heard during this reflection.

When most of the children have completed their illustrations, invite them to look at their pictures and describe what they saw or heard.

Engage in Discussion

• Jesus was teaching us to organize our time on earth because it is limited. We do not live forever on this earth, so we try to make each moment an important one. What are some of the important things in your life?

• What would Jesus say about the way you organize time, space, possessions, or the people in your life?

• How can we develop moral living patterns so that we make reasonable and intelligent decisions about organizing our time, space, and things?

Action Step

Look for a space or objects that you could organize this week. Take time to put things in order. Make a decision to put God first in your life.

Tips for Teaching this Skill

In our very busy world, learning to organize is important. We have to understand our limits so we can be the most successful in the time allowed.

The skill of organization is a generative self-discipline skill, meaning it will be difficult for children in kindergarten through high school to demonstrate on their own without prompting.

People begin to show that they can master this skill when they are in grade nine and up. Where early training has occurred, or a person has a natural tendency to organize, this skill may be performed at a much earlier age. Usually adults notice a youngster's inability to organize when they view lockers, desks, folders, or files.

When we organize time, space, people or things, we wait until we get a mental image of the way things are to be ordered. We think: what design, time-frame, schedule, grouping, or space will work the best?

The foundation of organizing time begins with children's ability to tell time. Assign tasks in short one- to ten-minute intervals to teach children how much they can accomplish in short increments of time.

The skill of organization can be structured

- linearly, when we use an agenda;

- circularly, as when we celebrate seasons and events that occur each year; and

- haphazardly, when we change schedules to accommodate unplanned, spontaneous events.

Remember that children in grades one through eight may need a system in order for them to get organized. Homework checks, activities in which they practice organizing time, making timelines and desk maps, outlining, conducting meetings, designing the class bulletin boards, building a family tree, and so on, will be excellent practices in which they can engage.

As you demonstrate the skill of organization, teach children the pitfalls. There are three pitfalls.

1. *Procrastination.* Putting off until later something we could do now.

2. *Escaping.* Daydreaming or doing something else that we feel more like doing.

3. *Deceiving yourself and others.* This happens when we don't take an honest look at the amount of time that will be needed for a task. Check the time or the amount of work needed to be done. This leads to using the excuse, "I ran out of time."

How It Works

The summer had just started, and Liz knew her two children would be spending many hours in the neighborhood swimming pool. The children were so excited the first day they went swimming. They talked all the way home about who they saw and what they did. It was obvious that they would really enjoy their time in the pool.

As they entered their house, the wet swimming towels were dumped right in the front entry way. Bathing suits landed on the kitchen table. Sandals and toys were spread out in various spots, from the kitchen all the way upstairs to the bedrooms. Liz took one look and decided this would be an excellent opportunity to teach the children how to organize their things on swimming days.

She brought the children down to the kitchen table and gave the older a pencil and paper, and she told the younger to listen and help with ideas. "I need you to make a reminder card for you and your brother so you will know what to do when we get home from swimming," she said. "There are six things I want you to remember. After you hear all

---

Skill Vocabulary

Use these phrases in class throughout the year to help reinforce the skill of organizing:

- Set your goals for the amount of time we have.

- Please describe a system we use to be organized.

- Will it be organized sequentially or randomly?

- What formal procedure can we use to conduct this meeting?

six, and have them listed on the card, we can talk about them."

1. When you come home, go right to the bathroom.

2. Wet towels go behind the door in the bathroom.

3. Rinse off your suits and yourself in the shower.

4. After you change clothes, the swimming suit should go out on the line to dry or be put over the shower rod.

5. All toys and swimming things will go in the plastic basket in the laundry room so we have them ready for our next trip.

6. All sandals and shoes will go on the small rug in the laundry room.

Liz waited as her daughter drew pictures and wrote a key word next to each item to help her brother remember what to do. After all the items had been recorded, Liz asked her son to use the card his sister had made to tell her six things they are to do when they come home from swimming. Her son knew all six without any help. In fact, when he needed time to think and his sister wanted to help him, he said, "I know, I know. Don't tell me."

The children were allowed to ask questions to clarify items and give their opinion of the steps. Teaching about how to organize space and things took about fifteen minutes. "It was the best fifteen minutes I spent that summer," said Liz.

Start the Year Organized

At the start of every new school year, educators and parents have a chance to set new goals and target areas for improvement. Modeling this behavior for children is an excellent way to show them how adults organize time, space, people, and things. As you model, intentionally name and tell youngsters the skill you are practicing.

Done well at the start of the school year this generative self-discipline skill can provide a much needed structure for children. Here are a few items that many adults find helpful in getting organized:

- A schedule for class sessions and home study.
- A place/space and supplies to do homework.
- Notebooks and other supplies, storage space,

lockers, briefcases, and desks.

- A method to help children learn the names of classmates, new staff members, support staff.
- Classroom duties.
- Procedures for handing in work and getting assignments when late or absent.
- A discipline cycle.
- Procedures and expectations for following rules.
- A grading system and ways to help children keep track of their progress.
- Rubrics that will be used in group work.
- A method so all children can have their questions answered.
- Routines for getting focused attention when needed.
- Study groups or student partners to help in the learning process.
- Data organizer that lists birthdays, home phone numbers, addresses, and other important information.

Be sure to add your own organization items to the list above to help you get started.

Activities

Teaching about Time

Invite intermediate grade students to help monitor younger children's understanding of time. They can do one or all of the following activities.

- Design a time quiz and check to see if children know how to read the time.
- Use pictures of a clock without hands. Give the younger person a time and ask them to draw in the hands.
- Use pictures of a clock with hands. Ask the person to write the time below the picture.
- Give the person a schedule. The schedule would list places in the school or home and times when they are to meet at that place. Be creative about the meeting place to

motivate younger children to become more aware of time.

Help Yourself Get Organized

There are five ways to help yourself organize time:

1. Do what you say you will do.

2. Play a game with yourself. See if you can set a time limit and get it done in that amount of time.

3. Race the clock. Beat your own time record in doing things.

4. Reward yourself. Take a break when you finish a task.

5. Tell a friend and ask them to encourage you to stick to your time schedules.

Games of Review

One activity that can be used in all classes to help children learn to organize time, space, people, and things is the art of reviewing. To create a review a person must organize objects, printed material, people, and time. Most child-led reviews can be completed in five to seven minutes. Here follow two sample reviews and the skills they address.

Tic Tac Toe

Organization of space. Nine chairs are placed in the front of the room in three rows of three. When you begin remind youngsters that, as they win, to seat themselves with their team in a line "tic-tac-toe" style.

Organization of materials. Students create questions from what they've learned to use as review for this game.

Organization of people. Decide if the game will be played row against row or if teams will be formed or if two individuals at a time will play against each other.

Organization of time. Tell the class how long the game will continue, for example, from five to eight minutes or until one team has won.

How the game is played. Children are asked questions by the leader. If the answer is correct, they take a seat on one of the nine chairs in the front of the room, again, seating themselves strategically. The

game continues as questions are asked alternately, one team to another. For example, if the boys represent the Xs and the girls the Os, whenever there are three boys or three girls seated across, down or diagonally that team is declared the winner.

Pick-a-word

Organization of time. Game can last five to ten minutes.

Organization of space. Determine board space. Use ten 8.5" x 11" sheets of paper or ten 4" x 5" sheets of paper for the playing cards. These will be taped to the board.

Organization of things. A key word or phrase to be reviewed is printed on the front of each card. Underneath each word or phrase is a number which will correspond to a point value. On the back of the card, there may be questions or clues to assist the person reviewing the item.

Organization of people. Determine teams or randomly select players. Organize how you will determine the first player, second, etc.

How the game is played. Children go to the board and select a card. Alone or with group help, they recite facts (between one to ten) related to the topic selected. If a word or topic has a point value of five, they can recite up to five facts and earn their team five points. If they are unable to recite five facts, they receive the number of points corresponding to the number of facts given. No deductions are made for incorrect answers. Once a word has been selected, no other team may select the card a second time.

Use Children's Literature

Rent Party Jazz, William Miller. When Sonny's mother loses her job in New Orleans during the Depression, Smiling Jack, a jazz musician, tells Sonny how to organize a rent party to raise the money they need. Shows how people make a difference when they work together.

The Dreamer, Cynthia Rylant. This is a beautifully illustrated story of the Divine Artist who dreamed the world, and all that dwells within it.

Harriet Tubman: Conductor on the Underground Railroad, Ann Lane Petry. This book tells how

Minty escaped North and made friends in Philadelphia. Her experience with the underground railroad encouraged her to go back and lead others to freedom.

Kate from Philadelphia: The Life of Saint Katharine Drexel for Children, Patricia Edward Jablonski. The daughter of a wealthy Philadelphia businessman, Kate gave up her riches to serve the Native American peoples of the western United States.

Use Music

Teach the song "I Am Organized," created by Jo Mersnick and sung to the tune of "London Bridge."

Organize your time today, time today, time today,
Be on time so you can say, I am organized!

Organize your desk today, desk today, desk today,
Make it neat so you can say, I am organized!

Organize your thoughts today, thoughts today,
* thoughts today.*
Think them out so you can say, I am organized!

Organize your work today, work today, work today,
Sort it out so you can say, I am organized.

Organize your plans today, plans today, plans today,
Schedule them so you can say, I am organized!

Poetry

Share this story with students and allow time for them to discuss how organizing their environment can be productive.

One Day at a Time

Jenna woke up feeling groggy and tired. She'd gone to bed at a decent time, but her mind had been spinning with excitement over the new room she would have in their new house. Her mom and dad had been talking about building a house during the next year, and Jenna couldn't wait to have a room of her own. She had been sharing a room with her sister, Stephanie, and lately things had gotten pretty miserable. As a matter of fact, they weren't even speaking except to say, "Get your clothes off my bed," or something similar.

Jenna just knew that a room of her own would solve the problem and that this feeling of depression would lift. "I know I'll be happy then," she promised herself.

—From *Heartwaves: Daily Meditations for Children*, written by Mary Bennett. Reprinted with permission.

Living in the future is a trap.
The only time I have is today!
I will make peace with my life as it is.

CHAPTER 12

Resolving Problems

So Zacchaeus ran ahead and climbed a sycamore tree to see him, because Jesus was going to pass that way. (Luke 19:4)

Reflection: How do I teach my students to use problem-solving in reconciling and maintaining right relationships with others?

The steps to resolving problems are

1. Recognize when a problem exists and attempt to identify the cause.

2. Explore all the facts.

3. Brainstorm possible ways to solve the conflict. Use "what if" thinking to explore the consequences.

4. Discard unrealistic solutions or any solution that will cause a problem for someone else.

5. Choose a solution, follow thorough, and evaluate the results.

Someone who knows how to resolve problems

- Identifies issues and concerns.
- Uses effective confrontation skills.
- Looks at the facts.
- Works with others to resolve issues.
- Keeps an open mind.
- Doesn't focus only on his or her side of the story.
- Doesn't succumb to gossip.
- Doesn't make problems for others.
- Doesn't close off possibilities.
- Doesn't get angry, pout, or refuse to work on the problem.

GUIDED REFLECTION

RESOLVING PROBLEMS

As we begin our reflection, prepare to listen to a reading from Scripture. Close your eyes. Take a deep breath and feel your body relax. Feel your feet and legs relax. Notice your arms and head feeling heavy. Your breathing has slowed down.

Picture Jesus walking along a dusty road on his way to a small village called Jericho. He is with his friends Peter, James, and John. As Jesus draws closer and closer to the village, he can hear the noise made by a crowd of people who have come out to see Jesus. Jesus has received great praise for the signs and wonders he works.

There is a tax collector and very wealthy man named Zacchaeus in the crowd. He knows Jesus is coming and yearns to see him, but he is too short and there are crowds of people in front of him. So Zacchaeus thinks for a minute. Many ideas run through his head as to what he can do. He chooses the one he thinks will be best.

Zacchaeus runs ahead of the crowd and climbs a sycamore tree. There he waits until Jesus passes by. Do you think this is a good solution to Zacchaeus' problem?

Picture in your mind what happens as Jesus comes closer to the spot where Zacchaeus is waiting. Keep this image in your mind as you slowly open your eyes. Now take out your reflection booklet and draw a picture of anything you saw or heard during this reflection.

When most of the children have completed their illustrations, invite them to look at their pictures and describe what they saw or heard.

Engage in Discussion

• Do you think Zacchaeus' plan was a good solution to his problem? Why or why not?
• Sometimes life presents us with problems, as it did for Zacchaeus, and we need to come up with a plan. Some problems are easier to fix than others. Brainstorm problems that might be easy to fix, and list them on the board. Let the children tell one or two ways to resolve each problem.
• How can we get closer to Jesus through resolving our problems?

Action Step

Invite youngsters to write in their reflection booklets about a problem that is more difficult to fix. Tell them you will read the problem and suggest one way it might be resolved. If they do not want to share the problem, tell them to fold the page so it will remain private and you will not read what they wrote.

Tips for Teaching this Skill

No matter what we do, we will always have problems. But what separates the good people from the great is the ability to overcome these obstacles.

Resolving problems is the fourth skill children are expected to do when they are disciplined. Along with listening, following instructions, and understanding the rules, resolving problems helps establish a safe environment in the classroom, when teachers attend to these skills.

The skill of resolving problems is a generative self-discipline skill, meaning it will be difficult for youngsters in kindergarten through high school to demonstrate on their own without prompting. People begin to show they can master this skill when they feel comfortable confronting others. Confrontation is a positive word that simply means "to come face to face."

When we resolve problems of mutual concern we wait until we can understand the problem from more than one point of view. We think: how can I state the problem from two different points of view? What solution would make us both winners?

To help children develop this skill, they can be taught some key principles.

- Problems cannot be solved by force but by talking.

- Time-out opportunities can be used to get ready to talk about a problem.

- People must work to solve a problem so the same thing doesn't occur the next time.

- Young children can be asked, "What will you do to show you are sorry?" when they know they have caused a problem for someone else.

- Children can be taught they cannot fix a problem by making a problem for someone else.

Contracts

One way to resolve problems is to write a contract. Teach students that a contract is an agreement to enter into mutual obligations. It includes a statement that clearly states the purpose of the contract. People who draw up contracts should be in a positive frame of mind and want to find a solution. They ask: "Do you want to find a new way to do things?" Persons forming a contract put it in writing

and list what each party agrees to do. They sign the contact and agree upon a renewal date.

Students should learn the principles of disagreements. Most important, it is okay to disagree. People who disagree are not strange or bad. When people disagree with an idea, it doesn't mean that the person's ideas are unimportant. People can disagree and still respect and trust each other.

When two people disagree it doesn't mean one is right and the other wrong, or that they are angry or don't like one another. Not all disagreements have to end with both people agreeing. You can agree to disagree. This is an important step to take in learning to resolve problems.

Conflict is often present when parties try to resolve problems. There are five basic methods adults use when resolving conflicts.

1. *Competition*. One person attempts to dominate.

2. *Accommodation*. One person gives up their position.

3. *Avoidance*. People need time because an issue is minor or too damaging to confront.

Skill Vocabulary

Use these phrases in class throughout the year to help reinforce the skill of resolving problems:

- Do you know how other children who have had this problem have fixed it?

- Do you want me to tell you how others with this problem have fixed it?

- If trying doesn't work, what will you be willing to do then?

- I understand what you are saying, and I think we can work it out.

- How does that information relate to our current problem?

- We can either talk about this issue now or later. Which do you prefer?

- I would like to practice some other ways to handle this problem if it comes up again.

- Take two minutes to think about what just happened and then we can talk about it.

- Problems cannot be solved by using violence but by talking.

4. *Compromise.* Both parties listen, negotiate, and are flexible. Each wins some and lose some in the discussion.

5. *Collaboration.* This is a win-win situation. Parties identify areas of agreement and disagreement. They look at alternatives and find mutually agreeable solutions.

These methods can be adapted and taught to children as an effective means of resolving conflict.

Consequences

Finally, children should understand that consequences are a result of problem situations. These are the criteria for consequences:

- Every action has a resulting reaction.
- Consequences are meant to teach lessons.
- In most cases, a consequence can be negotiable.

There are three types of consequences: natural and logical, self-imposed, and adult-imposed. Adult-imposed consequences are given when a serious violation of another's rights has occurred, either because someone is in physical or psychological danger, someone is abusive in tone or gesture, or someone is out of control and cannot be reasoned with.

Consequences are also imposed by adults when a cue or verbal correction does not help a person correct their inappropriate behaviors, or a youngster reaches a certain step in the classroom disciplinary procedures.

In other cases a person may become aware that they are having difficulty following procedures or rules. They can make a decision to change. The plan of action they choose is called a self-imposed consequence. A self-imposed or an adult-imposed consequence may be easy for one person but difficult for someone else. But when someone is willing to take the consequences for their actions, that shows they want to take control over their life.

Here are a few sample consequences that can be used with your class. The student can:

- Exclude him or herself when the class does a special project. He or she can offer to do some task that will help the class or the school environment during that time.
- List five things the child can do to show understanding of the rule that was not followed.
- List ten responsibilities students have to the teacher and to one another in the classroom.
- List his or her seven best qualities, then share the list with another adult. The student tells the other person what he or she did and why the student did this project, and asks for the adult's advice.

How It Works

Two sophomores and senior were caught taking doughnuts from a food tray that had been put out for guests visiting the school that day. Willing to own up to what they had done, the students went to talk to the teacher who had prepared the food.

The teacher, knowing that all three young men had already had a full year's course on learning to be self-disciplined, began to model and use the skills in the confrontation that ensued.

After the initial greetings and handshakes, the teacher turned to the senior and said, "Tell me what happened." The senior, with a flair for drama, began, "Oh, that French roast coffee you put out smelled so good, I was lured to the window. When I saw the doughnuts temptation got the better of me and I took a few. But I am here to tell you that I am sorry."

Without reacting to what the senior had said, the teacher asked the two sophomores what had happened. The first replied, "Well, we were on our way over to take a few doughnuts, too, but before we could grab some the senior was caught. Even though we didn't take any of the doughnuts, we were blamed for taking them, too."

The teacher took a moment to distinguish between what she was feeling and the facts she had just heard. In a calm voice she thanked the young men for their willingness to state the problem, then asked, "How will you make recompense?"

"Excuse me?" said the senior.

"How will you pay back what you took?" replied the teacher. "You just ate part of the breakfast I had prepared for my guests. I would like you to replace what you took."

"I can't do that," said the senior. "We're not allowed off campus during the school day."

The sophomores tried to be helpful. "Can he replace the doughnuts with something from the school vending machines?" said one.

"That would be fine," said the teacher."I'd like you to do that as soon as possible. Is this agreeable to you?"

The senior shook his head reluctantly. "Yeah, I guess that would be fine."

The teacher shook hands with all three of the students, and thanked them for their help in resolving the problem. She had kept the conversation neutral and did not pass judgment or blame. She simply focused on how the problem would be fixed and on who would fix it.

Activities

Steps to Using Consequences in the Classroom

There are three steps that help students recognize and correct inappropriate behavior in the classroom. They are:

1. Select a consequence from the ones shown on the consequence card (or other consequences that you have devised for your class).

2. Write a letter to his or her parents or the principal describing what you did and how you plan to fix it.

3. Deliver the letter. Discuss the contents. Ask a parent to sign it and return it to the teacher.

When children cannot change their behavior with just a verbal reminder, they are instructed to select a consequence from the card below. If the misbehavior continues, they move to step two and draw or write a letter to their parents or principal. This letter stays on their desk. If their disruptive behavior continues, they move to step three, and the letter is delivered and discussed with an adult.

CONSEQUENCE CARD

Name: _____

If I interrupt the class by breaking a rule I will:

1. Write an apology

2. Miss a privilege.

3. Miss ❑ five ❑ ten ❑ fifteen minutes of free time.

4. Do some act to show I am sorry.

Is It Tattling?

Primary-grade children feel a moral obligation to report to adults when rules are broken. When children are ages five to seven, this situation can be handled very simply by using one of these approaches.

- Politely thank the child for reporting. Do nothing else.
- Ask the child "Are you telling me because you want me to do something or just to let me know?" If they want you to do something, encourage them to work with you to solve the problem.
- Create an "I witness," box and let children draw or print the problems they notice on 5" x 8" cards and place them in the box. Periodically open the box and review the concerns they have by talking about each item.

Teach young children that they are accountable for their actions by helping them understand the difference between appropriate and inappropriate actions. Use a teaching mode that will help children learn the acceptable classroom behaviors. Teach them that there are consequences when inappropriate actions occur.

Sample Procedures for Teaching Consequences

Consequences are a part of resolving problems. It is important to teach children what will happen when rules are not followed. Here follow several different approaches to classroom discipline that can be used throughout the year. You may find it helpful to alternate different methods depending on the problem being addressed.

Approach 1

Step 1

Select one of the following:

- Give the child a cue that he or she is misbehaving. Use proximity, and move closer to the youngster.
- Ask the child a question.
- Lower your voice as a signal for children to focus on listening.
- Redirect student behavior.

Step 2

Select one of the following:

- Give a verbal warning.
- Make an appointment to see the child later.
- Have the child take time out in the session.
- Tell the child he or she is losing involvement in an activity or privilege.

Step 3

- Have the child make a plan. They can ask themselves: What did I do? What could I do differently next time?
- Call a parent.

Step 4

- Meet with a parent
- Draw up a contract.

Step 5

- Meet with the Director of Religious Education.

Approach 2

1. Give the child one chance to correct him or herself. If he or she does not correct the behavior, the following steps are taken, in order.

2. Interaction between child and teacher.

3. Notification of parents (written notice, phone call, student notifies).

4. Verbal contact with parents (child and teacher or principal speak with parents).

5. Meeting with principal, parents, student. Principal describes the situation and receives a commitment from the child. Parents are notified regarding the next two steps.

6. Second meeting with parents. Child will be removed from class. Parents, student, teacher, principal will arrive at a mutually agreed upon group behavior plan.

The next steps need to be coordinated with the disciplinary procedures of the parish faith formation program or of the school.

7. In-school suspension (can be repeated).

8. Out of school suspension (1-5 days).

9. Expulsion is the final step.

Approach 3

This plan was developed and is used by various teachers who work with junior high and high school teens. Under each of the four steps listed below, options are given. Students are taught that any one of the options might be used by different teachers. Because teachers prefer to work with youngsters in different ways, and because class settings lend themselves to different forms of accountability, options are given.

1. The first time a teen misbehaves, depending upon the behavior one of the following will take place.

- The catechist or teacher will remind the teen with a look, or will use the teen's name.
- The catechist might also stand near the young person or ask him or her a question.
- The catechist could also change his or her tone of voice, or redirect the teen's behavior.

2. The second time the teen misbehaves, he or she may be given a verbal warning, or the catechist may choose to table the matter. The catechist could also make an appointment to talk with the young person, or tell him or her that this is the last warning.

3. The third time a teen misbehaves, the catechist or teacher may require interaction with parent(s), or interaction with the catechist or teacher after class. The catechist or teacher may decide to draw up a contract with the teen, or to issue a demerit, or to deprive them of involvement in an activity.

4. The fourth instance of misbehavior usually requires interaction with the parent and the DRE or the principal.

Approach 4

A Wait, Think, Plan card, such as the one shown here, can be used when a child has been given a verbal reminder and is not able to get him or herself under control. Place one of these cards on the young-

Wait

Think

Plan

1. What skill were you not using when this card was given to you?

2. How should you act if you are using this skill?

3. What is your plan for rejoining the class?

ster's desk. This is a signal that they should take a seat and sit down and think about their actions.

The catechist checks back in several minutes to confer with the youngster and learn the plan he or she will use to come back with the class. The child can then rejoin the group. If the disruption occurs a second time, they are handed the WTP card and must now write the answer to several questions that are listed on the back of the card. The card is sent home and signed by a parent.

Time-Out

Giving children a time-out can be a very productive strategy. It gives them a chance to separate fact from feeling (a difficult self-discipline skill) and to calm down. They can think about what happened and write or draw their side of the story. They can set a goal for what they plan to do the next time.

The most important step in using a time-out is the dialogue that occurs between the child and the adult. Some people find it helpful to have children complete the answers to these questions in writing or verbally if they are sent to a time-out.

• Why do I think I was sent to time-out?

• What is my side of the story?

• What do I think should happen next?

Be very careful not to send a child into time-out—or use any disciplinary action, for that matter—simply because you are tired or in a bad mood.

Three Ways to Solve Problems

Teach intermediate grade students that problems can be handled in one of three ways: passively, aggressively, or assertively. Help children understand the difference between these three approaches. Discuss situations such as the following. Encourage an assertive approach whenever possible.

A parent tells you your messy room must be cleaned before you can go outside. What are you likely to do?

a) Pay a brother or sister to do it for you (passive approach).

b) Begin to clean your room right away or negotiate about the time when you plan to clean your room (assertive approach).

c) Get angry and yell, "You're not fair. It's my room and I like it messy. Why can't I leave it the way I like it?" (aggressive approach).

Keep Records

Enlarge and reproduce the following form to help children learn better ways to resolve problems. Keep copies of the written plan in each child's folder.

I CAN MAKE A PLAN

1. I did not follow a rule. This is what I did.

_____

2. How did this affect:

The teacher? _____

The students? _____

Me? _____

3. Three things I could do to help myself are:

a) _____

b) _____

c) _____

4. The next time I will:

_____

_____

Student _____

Date _____

Teacher _____

Use Children's Literature

Fables, Arnold Lobel. Twenty original fables by Lobel tell about an array of animal characters, from crocodile to ostrich, who figure out their problems. Each tale teaches a lesson or moral. Caldecott, 1981.

Mrs. Frisby and the Rats of NIMH, Robert. C. O'Brien. Having no one to help her with her problem, a widowed mouse visits the rats of NIMH who come up with a great solution to save her son Timothy. In turn, Mrs. Frisby does them a great service and saves their lives. Newbery, 1972.

Sweet Clara and the Freedom Quilt, Deborah Hopkinson. Clara gets help from others on the location of rivers, houses, and landmarks when she stitches a quilt with a map pattern that guides her and many others to freedom. This brave slave girl plays an unusual part in the Underground Railroad.

Through My Eyes: The Autobiography of Ruby Bridges. Ruby, the first black pupil to attend a formerly segregated school in 1960, tells her own story combining adult commentary, news reports of the time, and personal memories of what the experience was like for her as a six-year-old-child.

Use Poetry

In this poem used in primary grades, children discuss taking ownership for problems. They learn that using the phrase, "I don't know how this happened" rarely resolves a problem.

I Don't Know How This Happened

Don't ask me how this happened,
'Cause, I really do not know
How this stupid soda bottle
Got stuck on my big toe.
I was minding my own business.
I didn't do a thing.
I was sitting here real quiet.
When all of a sudden...Ping!
I looked to see what happened
And saw the bottle there.
I don't know where it came from.
I really don't. I swear.

—*Illustration and poem by Christine Ryktarsyk*

CHAPTER 13

Initiating Solutions

And when they could not bring him to Jesus because of the crowd, they removed the roof above him;
and...let down the mat on which the paralytic lay. (Mark 2:4)

Reflection: How do I help my students develop the skills to bring the gospel message to the world?

Steps toward initiating a solution

1. Always go to the source of the problem.

2. Talk it through with a neutral person if needed.

3. Make an appointment if it is necessary to speak with an adult or peer.

4. Put what needs to be said in writing for clarity.

5. Have in mind the results we would like to happen.

Tip: We cannot fix a problem by making a problem for anyone else.

Someone who knows how to initiate a solution

• Is willing to take the first step.

• Asks for help if needed.

• Makes an appointment.

• Doesn't talk behind someone's back.

• Doesn't ignore a problem.

• Doesn't confront others inappropriately.

GUIDED REFLECTION

INITIATING SOLUTIONS

As we begin our reflection, prepare to listen to a reading from Scripture. Close your eyes. Take a deep breath and feel your body relax. Feel your feet and legs relax. Notice your arms and head feeling heavy. Your breathing has slowed down.

Start your reflection by picturing Jesus in a quaint little home in the town of Capernaum. Friends and acquaintances heard that Jesus was home from his travels. They started to visit him, and before long the house was crowded with people. The door to his house was blocked because of the huge crowd of followers.

There was a paralyzed man who wanted to see Jesus. He was hoping Jesus would help him. As hard as he tried, he couldn't even get up to the door to shout at Jesus. There were four men who saw the expression on the man's face and recognized how important it would be for him to see Jesus. They took the first step to initiate a solution to the man's problem.

They got a sturdy mat and some ropes and carried the mat and the man up to the top of the house. Once they were on the roof, they made an opening in the straw that covered the house. When they broke through and could see the people below, they slowly lowered the man on the mat. Picture the paralyzed man on the mat slowly coming through the roof. What are the people below doing? What does Jesus do? What expression does the paralyzed man have on his face now?

Keep this image in your mind as you slowly open your eyes. Now take out your reflection booklet and draw a picture of anything you saw or heard during this reflection.

When most of the children have completed their illustrations, invite them to look at their pictures and describe what they saw or heard.

Engage in Discussion

• Do you think the initiative the four men took was beneficial? What does Jesus do when he sees the man? Tell students that Jesus always made people feel welcomed. He often invited them by saying, "Come, follow me." How can we model Jesus in this behavior?

• Talk with the students about some helpful tips they can use when they take the first step to resolve a problem, using the steps shown on the previous page.

• How can we invite the Holy Spirit to inspire our efforts in initiating solutions?

Action Step

Invite youngsters to write about a time when they took the first step to resolve a problem. The problem may have been theirs or that of someone they knew. Direct them to look for problems that are in need of a solution, and to use the four men in the story as their model. The men acted as soon as they recognized that someone needed help.

Tips for Teaching this Skill

Many times we encounter difficult situations. Each time this occurs, it is important to be creative and insightful in finding an answer.

Taking the first step to initiate a solution to a problem is a generative self-discipline skill, meaning it will be difficult for youngsters in kindergarten through high school to demonstrate on their own without prompting.

When we take the initiative to solve a problem we wait until we notice that a problem exists. We think: how can I name the problem so others will understand it? What solution will make all parties winners? What outcome do I expect to occur?

People show that they can master this skill when they begin to feel comfortable confronting others. A person who takes the first step to initiate a solution to a problem should be clear about what they would like to see happen as a result of this confrontation. Some possible outcomes are:

- The other party will agree with me.
- I will agree with the other party.
- We will compromise.
- We will agree to disagree.
- We will both agree to something entirely different.

Solving problems is a matter of opening minds!

How It Works

The staff at St. Monica's worked hard at the beginning of the school year to develop a self-discipline behavior code that would make the learning environment more pleasant for everyone. They had a list of twelve actions that all teachers agreed they would try to model for one year. Items on their list included using their social skills to make volunteers and substitute teachers feel welcome, and using their organizational skills to outline a schedule to have the entryway bulletin board changed monthly.

A member of the staff volunteered to type the completed list. She made copies for each teacher to frame and put in their classrooms. The teachers were amazed that just doing this simple activity built a collaborative spirit among the group.

In March Ms. Abts, one of the fifth grade teachers, found out that a peer had been talking about her in the faculty room. The comments were innocent enough, and they were based on facts. Ms. Abts was upset, however, that others did not come to her to verify the information. Confrontation was not her favorite activity and yet she knew she had to confront what happened.

After a few hours of soul searching, Ms. Abts knew what she would do. She went over to the behavior code she had previously hung on her wall. Taking it down, she went down the hall to speak to the peer.

Facing the teacher, she asked, "Is this a good time for us to visit for a few minutes?" When the peer said it was, Ms. Abts started by showing her the code. "We agreed to model the self-discipline skill of problem solving by going to the source of the problem. I need to talk to you about what I have heard," she began.

Both teachers felt better when the confrontation was over. Ms. Abts confessed this was the first time she had had the courage to confront a peer. The other teacher also felt as if this was a first. "Last year when things like this happened, we just whispered behind people's backs, leaving everyone with a very unprofessional and uncomfortable feeling," she said. "I know this wasn't easy for you. I'm really glad you confronted me, because I was wrong in not coming to you first."

When approached correctly, initiating a solution to a problem will be a self-discipline skill people can use for a lifetime.

Skill Vocabulary

Use these phrases in class throughout the year to help reinforce the skill of initiating solutions:

- You can take the first step to fix this problem or I can. Which do you choose?
- You cannot fix a problem by making a problem for someone else.
- The outcome may not be what you expect. Are you still willing to work on a solution?
- Thank you for making the first move to resolve this problem.
- If I fixed the problem this is what I would do, but you have the first move.
- How will you make recompense?

Activities

Explore How Others Handle Problems

Adults and older children can explore the elements of initiating solutions by discussing problems and ways to handle problems. Try this game. Write each of the phrases below on a slip of paper, then put the slips into a container. Divide the class into groups of five or six people each. Invite one person from each group to pull a slip from the container and finish the sentence. Allow discussion to flow freely before moving to the next person in the group.

- I'll never forget the time...
- I probably should have told you this before...
- I need to tell you the truth about...
- The most difficult problem I have had to face is...
- When I face problems I usually...
- If I have trouble with someone I usually...
- I get angry when...
- When I am angry I usually....

End the discussion by inviting each person to tell one thing they learned about themselves or a member of the group during this session.

Taking the First Step

Discuss with students how difficult it is to make the first move when there is a problem. In their reflection journal or on a separate piece of paper, invite them to write or illustrate a time when a problem could not be solved because no one was willing to make the first move.

When the students are done, ask for a few volunteers to share their stories with the class. After listening to the stories, together list three things that would help someone make the first move and three things that would make it difficult.

Challenge students to look for opportunities to initiate solutions during the week and report back on what they observed.

Negotiate for What You Want

An important step in taking the initiative to resolve problems is the ability to negotiate for what is desired. Negotiation can start at any age. The use of a simple contract can help children learn this skill. Contracts can be written when children want a privilege, want to purchase something, or need help in tending to their assigned responsibilities. This month challenge each student to work with you to negotiate a contract. A simple contract might read:

I, (name), will do my assignments and homework for each class this month. When I accomplish this, I will be allowed to skip one day's assignments and/or homework.

At the end of the week or month, evaluate each contract. Discuss together:

- Did the contract help? How?
- Did you accomplish your goal? How can we work together to help you accomplish your goal?
- Are there other problems at home or school or with your friends you could resolve by using a contract?

Use the Same Vocabulary

Develop some common expressions that youngsters can use when they want to resolve issues. Put these on a card and keep it for future reference, or write them on a poster and display it in your classroom.

- Let's explore the alternatives.
- Put yourself in my place.
- Can we live with the things we cannot change?
- Can you help me understand your reasons?
- Is there a solution we haven't thought about yet?
- Should we ask other people for some ideas?
- How can we resolve this so we both can come out winners?

Make Nonjudgmental Statements

Teach children to use nonjudgmental statements when they are trying to initiate a solution to a problem.

1. State a specific behavior: "Right now you are rolling your eyes and you have folded your arms." or "When you use that gesture, tone of voice, those words...."

2. Use an "I feel" statement rather than a "You are" statement: "I feel put off." "I am offended."

3. Give a reason: "It takes two people to work things out. Is this a good time to talk about this issue?" "It shows disrespect for yourself and those who have to listen to you."

Act as a Resource Person

We can be resource persons by taking the children's problems seriously and asking what they think they might do about them. "That is a problem. Have you thought about how you will fix it?"

Then we might offer alternatives: "Would you like me to tell you how others in your situation have fixed their problem?" We should then honor their response. If they say, "No," let them think about it on their own. If they say "Yes," we can suggest at least three things they could do.

Help them keep in mind this one rule: you cannot fix a problem by making a problem for anyone else.

Think Before You Confront

Recall that confrontation simply means to come face-to-face. People practice this skill in a productive manner when they:

- use an appropriate tone of voice
- calm themselves
- describe what they see or hear without making any judgments
- make appointments to speak in private rather than confront in front of others
- put issues in writing and make an agenda
- express strong feelings using appropriate language and body postures
- put things on hold if feelings are too strong
- use skill language that is neutral
- avoid sarcasm and intimidation.

When you need to make the first step to confront someone, it is often helpful to reflect on the following questions:

- Does this person's behavior affect me directly? Has it happened more than once and is it likely to happen again?
- Is this a good time to confront this issue?
- Would this issue ever resolve itself?
- Am I the best person to address this issue?
- Is there someone else who might be a better person to confront this issue?

- Are my feelings about the issue grounded in the here and now?
- Am I ready to let this matter drop once I've expressed my feelings and asked for what I need or want?

Using Children's Literature

Julie of the Wolves, Jean Craighead George. Miyax is lost in the Alaskan wilderness. She uses her father's Eskimo training, and struggles day by day to survive. Slowly she is accepted by a pack of Arctic wolves who help her stay alive. Newbery Medal, 1973.

The Great Kapok Tree: A Tale of the Amazon Rain Forest, Lynne Cherry. The kapok tree is part of the rain forest canopy. When a man tries to chop down the Great Kapok Tree, the community of animals take turns whispering in his ear all that will happen if he destroys their home.

Raven: A Trickster Tale from the Pacific Northwest, Gerald McDermott. Raven decides to restore light to the world, but first he must disguise himself as a child to get close to the light. Caldecott Honor, 1994.

Wilfrid Gordon McDonald Partridge, Mem Fox. Wilfrid tries to discover the meaning of memory so he can help an elderly friend remember the past.

Initiate a Solution to a Parish Need

Idea submitted by Chris Broslavick and Tony Pichler.
Review some guidelines for initiating solutions with
your class.

- Always go to the source of the problem.
- Talk it through with a neutral person.
- When you need to speak to an adult make an
  appointment.
- Put what you want to say in writing.
- Be clear about the results you hope for.

Divide the class into groups of three or four students. Distribute paper and pencils to each small
group.

Instruct each group to brainstorm various needs
of your parish or school. These might include items
such as child care for young children, a food pantry
for the poor and hungry, or transportation for
young people to religious education classes or field
trips. Next, have the groups choose one item from
their list. Using the criteria for initiating solutions,
ask the students to map out the strategies they
might use to create solutions to the various issues.

After the groups have had a sufficient amount of
time to talk through the issues, invite a representa-
tive from each group to share the issue and possible
solutions with the class. As a class, select one concern to work on. Determine who will carry out each
part of the process, realizing that it may take weeks
to actually resolve the issue. Allow time to report on
the issue weekly until a resolution is found.

CHAPTER 14

Separating Fact from Feeling

Mary stood weeping outside the tomb. (John 20:11)

Reflection: How do I help my students use their conscience to decide what is moral?

Steps to separating fact from feeling

1. Admit to ourselves how we feel. Name our feelings.

2. Don't blame ourselves for our feelings. Feelings are neither good nor bad.

3. Talk about our feelings with the person best able to help us with the situation.

4. Start our sentences with phrases such as, "I feel...," "When you...," and "Because...."

5. Put a conversation on hold until we have sorted through the facts and the feelings.

Someone who can distinguish fact from feeling

• Describes their feelings.

• Combines feelings with the facts.

• Sorts out how they feel.

• Defines facts.

• Doesn't ignore facts or feelings.

• Doesn't blow up when upset.

• Doesn't act on emotion.

GUIDED REFLECTION

SEPARATING FACT FROM FEELING

As we begin our reflection, prepare to listen to a reading from Scripture. Close your eyes. Take a deep breath and feel your body relax. Feel your feet and legs relax. Notice your arms and head feeling heavy. Your breathing has slowed down.

Today, we are going to reflect on what happened after Jesus died on the cross. Picture two men taking Jesus down from the cross and wrapping him in a blanket. They carry him to a tomb that was carved out of the side of a mountain. They careful lay him in the tomb. When they leave, the two roll a large stone over the front of the tomb to seal the area. The men are sure Jesus will be safe here.

The night passes. Early the next morning, Mary of Magdala visits the tomb. As she gets closer, she sees that the large stone was moved away from the entrance. She peeks inside and finds that the tomb is empty. Picture Mary's face as she realizes Jesus is gone.

Mary runs to tell the apostle, Simon Peter, that the tomb is empty. She tells Peter that Jesus did what he promised. He is risen and is alive even though he had been dead three days earlier. Simon and another disciple run to the tomb and look inside. It is empty! Stunned, they return home.

Mary stays outside the tomb weeping. She is unaware of the things around her, but eventually she notices a gardener. When the gardener looks at her, he says, "Mary!" She turns and gasps, exclaiming, "Rabbouni," which means Teacher. Mary recognizes Jesus in the gardener.

Picture Mary of Magdala in your mind. What was she feeling? What did she know to be true about Jesus? Keep this image in your mind as you slowly open your eyes. Now take out your reflection booklet and draw a picture of anything you saw or heard during this reflection.

When most of the children have completed their illustrations, invite them to look at their pictures and describe what they saw or heard.

Engage in Discussion

• What was Mary feeling? What facts did she know about Jesus?
• Tell the children that when people feel many different ways at the same time we call it mixed emotions. Mixed emotions cause people to run away, hide, cry, get embarrassed, giggle, or get angry. It is helpful at such times to talk to yourself and admit, "I am experiencing mixed emotions and do not know how I am really feeling." Make a decision to talk about your mixed emotions with someone who can help you sort them out. Who might you go to for help?
• Talk about ways that we can trust our intuition, and believe in what is not always visible to the eye.

Action Step

Invite youngsters to write in their reflection booklets about a time when they experienced mixed emotions and to tell what they did when this happened.

Tips for Teaching this Skill

Separating fact from feeling is like hanging between two cliffs. You can't hold both, but must pick one. Keeping your head clear so you can see the facts is the key.

Distinguishing fact from feeling is a generative self-discipline skill, meaning it will be difficult for youngsters in kindergarten through high school to demonstrate on their own without prompting. Children in grades six to ten are at the optimum age to learn about and practice this skill.

When we distinguish fact from feeling we wait until we have neutralized strong emotions. We think: what name can I put on my feelings? What causes me to have these feelings?

Making decisions knowing the facts and our feelings, using our head and our heart is a skill people will use for a lifetime. You can teach the steps of this skill by helping students to name their feelings and then describe how those feelings affect both their body and mind. You can help them learn to trust both comfortable and uncomfortable feelings, to combine the feelings with the facts, and to make a decision to act in a way that considers both.

Skill Vocabulary

Use these phrases in class throughout the year to help reinforce the skill of separating fact from fiction:

• What are your strongest feelings right now?

• Can you name what you are feeling?

• What are the facts?

• Delay your impulsiveness until we have both the facts and the feelings sorted out.

• When you_____, I feel_____ because_____.

• Is there a neutral person you can talk to about this issue?

• I'm having trouble separating fact from feeling right now. I need more time to think about this. I'll get back to you later.

• Where does the feeling hit you inside—in your head, your eyes, mouth, throat, heart stomach, feet, or somewhere else?

How It Works

Holy Rosary School has been teaching the students about the fifteen self-discipline skills for over seven years. Many of the students who began in kindergarten are now in the junior high. They have grown up on the skills and know skill language well. They know that both the adults as well as the children are working to demonstrate the skills in their daily life. Teachers encourage children to use skill language and to enter into a collaborative adventure as they both practice the skills.

One day, Matt, a junior high student, was sent to the office to visit the principal. This was Matt's third visit in less than two weeks and the principal was very disappointed to see him again. She knew this visit meant that Matt would have to be given stronger consequences as a result of his behavior. A contract would have to be drawn up to place stipulations on his behavior if he wanted to stay at Holy Rosary.

Matt, too, was disappointed in his behavior. He looked at his principal's face and very quietly said, "Mrs. Jones, do you need some time to separate fact from feeling?" Mrs. Jones nodded. She noted how well the staff had taught Matt to recognize when other people are affected by his behavior. "Yes, Matt," she said. "In fact, I think you had better just take a seat and give me some time to figure out what I need to say to you."

Activities

Where Do You Feel It?

To help young children identify where feelings localize themselves, use a routine checklist when they are feeling strongly one way or another. You might ask. "Where do you feel your anger? In your head, your eyes, your cheeks, your mouth, your throat, your hands, your chest, your stomach, your legs, your feet, or somewhere else?"

Then ask: "What does it feel like?" Find descriptive words to tell others what the feeling is like. In response to where a person might feel anger, you might hear. "I feel the anger in my eyes. It feels as though my eyes have x-ray vision and I can see through things."

Develop Feeling Cards

The following card was created by fifth graders and posted by the pencil sharpener. Here students are learning about two skills. It is a social skill to know when to make noise so others are not disturbed. Also, unnecessary noise can cause others to experience strong negative feelings.

Invite children to create other feeling cards that represent some of the feelings they experience during the school day.

Mixed Emotions

Identify some of the things people do when they are experiencing mixed emotions. They run away, hide, cry, freeze, get embarrassed, are unable to find words to describe what they are feeling, giggle, or get angry.

Teach self-talk, with statements such as, "I am experiencing mixed emotions and do not know how I am feeling." Encourage students to talk about their mixed emotions with someone who might be able to help sort them out.

Show students the ladder of emotions. Teach them what people who cannot distinguish fact from feeling do when they have problems. Talk about what people who know how to use this skill can do.

| Work the problem together |
| Talk to a friend or adult |
| Deal directly |
| Think of other's feelings and needs |
| Calm your mind and muscles |
| Escape, run, hide |
| Build up feelings on the inside |
| Cry, yell, use inappropriate language |
| Tease, name call, sarcasm, rudeness |
| Damage or steal property |
| Hurt self or others physically |

Use Poetry

Share this poem with your youngsters and ask them to evaluate it.

My Secret Fear

No one knows my secret fear
So please don't tell a soul.
I have this terrible, nagging fear
That I'll fall down a hole.

The hole will be dark and deep and dank,
And I will fall and fall,
Picking up slimy, creepy critters
Whenever I brush the wall.

When I finally, finally reach the bottom
I'll hit with a deafening thud!
And when I try to stand up,
I'll find that I can't
'Cause I'm up to my hips in mud!

I'll rock and I'll jump and I'll squirm all around.
Trying to get myself free.
But in the end, 'm afraid it will be
The dark hole, the mud, and...me.

—Christine Ryktarsyk

Use Music

Teach children the following song created by Jo Mersnick, and sung to the tune of "Itsy Bitsy Spider."

Facts and Feelings

Don't let your FEEL-INGS rule you to-day.
Don't let your FEEL-INGS get in the way.
Stop and think, Seek out the facts, Dis-cov-er the truth, Then you can act.

CHAPTER 15

Making Sacrifices to Serve Others

She out of her poverty has put in everything she had, all she had to live on. (Mark 12:44)

Reflection: How do I teach my students to make sacrifices and be of service to others?

The steps to making a sacrifice are

1. Compare things or actions according to the needs of others or what is best for most people. In doing so we think: "What does the gospel teach us about this?"

2. Decide what to keep and which to let go of.

3. Focus on the satisfaction of making a choice for the greater good or for the benefit of someone other than ourselves.

A sacrifice is an act of giving up something in order to gain something equally as good or better.

Someone who makes sacrifices

- Seeks ways to be of service.
- Notices the needs of others.
- Understands the meaning of "the greater good."
- Makes a conscious choice to serve.
- Lives with their decision.
- Doesn't think only of self.
- Isn't "me" centered.
- Doesn't only focus on his or her own wants.
- Doesn't drift along letting circumstances and time influence his or her choices.
- Doesn't nurture regrets.

GUIDED REFLECTION

As we begin our reflection, prepare to listen to a reading from Scripture. Close your eyes. Take a deep breath and feel your body relax. Feel your feet and legs relax. Notice your arms and head feeling heavy. Your breathing has slowed down.

Today, we will picture Jesus in the Jewish temple. The temple has tall pillars and many altars. People are buying doves and other animals to use as a sacrifice. They are coming and going, offering their sacrifices, praying, and then leaving. Jesus is standing near the doorway so he can greet people as they come in. At the entrance to the temple there is a collection basket. Many rich people come to the temple and are generous. They put in large sums of money. Some smile broadly, and you can tell they are proud of what they are about to do.

MAKING SACRIFICES TO SERVE OTHERS

As Jesus watches, he sees a poor widow come through the temple doorway. She reaches into her pocket and finds two small coins which are worth only a few cents. The disciples that are with Jesus notice her, too. Jesus tells them: "This poor widow put in more than all the other contributors to the collection."

"How can this be?" the people wonder. "She has contributed all the money that she has to live on," says Jesus, "while the others gave from their surplus wealth."

Picture this poor woman in your mind. She has nothing, yet she is so generous with the little she has. Somehow she knows that all of the things we have in this world are given to us by God. Think about all the pictures you have seen. In this meditation, select one scene that stands out. Keep this image in your mind as you slowly open your eyes. Now take out your reflection booklet and draw a picture of anything you saw or heard during this reflection.

When most of the children have completed their illustrations, invite them to look at their pictures and describe what they saw or heard.

Engage in Discussion

• What was Jesus trying to teach his disciples?

• What can we learn from this story?

• Name someone you know who made a sacrifice like the woman in the story. What did they do?

• Describe a random act of kindness done for another.

• How can we learn to sacrifice some of what is important to us in order to better serve God and other people?

Action Step

In your reflection booklet, list some sacrifices you could do this week. Pick one to focus on and make sure you do it during the week.

Tips for Teaching This Skill

All of us are wonderfully blessed. But every one of us is called to make sacrifices to help others. That way we return some of what we are given. Serving others or making sacrifices is a generative self-discipline skill, meaning it will be difficult for children in kindergarten through high school to demonstrate on their own without prompting. Students in grades six to ten are at the optimum age for learning about and practicing this skill.

When we make sacrifices and serve others, we wait to have our needs or desires met. We think: "What am I willing to let go of or give up so life will be better for me and/or others?"

Remember that primary children will understand this skill more by the adult's manner in talking about the skill than from a conceptual basis. For example, the catechist or teacher or parent says: "When you shared your cookie with someone who did not have one, you made my heart feel really warm. You made a sacrifice and that is the highest self-discipline skill a person can do." When the adult says this with conviction, the child will sense the meaning of making a sacrifice and will know he or she has done something very good.

Primary grade children learn that when they choose to do any self-discipline skill, there will be a benefit to themselves as well as others. This concept sets the foundation for the skill of making sacrifices.

Skill Vocabulary

• What are you willing to give up? What will you gain?

• What two valuable items are in competition here?

• That action was "super fair."

• Not everyone will be able to practice this skill.

• I need a volunteer.

• The kind of volunteer I need is someone who won't get the giggles when they get in front of the room, who likes to role play, who can take this task seriously, and so on.

• This isn't a matter of fairness. I'm asking you to think about the needs of others now.

TO MAKE A SACRIFICE A PERSON MIGHT

1. Recognize that he/she may not be able to hold on to two or more valuable things at the same time.

2. Compare the things according to certain parameters (the example of Jesus and the saints, the needs of others, which is best for the most people, etc.).

3. Decide which of the things they will choose and which they will let go of.

4. Admit that it is difficult to let one of the things go.

5. Focus on the satisfaction of their choice for the greater good and/or for the benefit of someone other than themselves.

6. Live with the decision and avoid nurturing regrets.

7. Accept compliments that may come from others because they have seen that person make a sacrifice.

Look for opportunities to name sacrifices you notice others are making.

Children in grades three to five will understand this skill when you use a term that may be familiar to them. To sacrifice means "being super fair." They can brainstorm actions that they would consider to be super fair. Use this list to identify persons who demonstrate the skill of making sacrifices. A sacrifice is an act of giving something up in order to gain something equally as good or better.

The steps adults go through to make a sacrifice can be posted for older students to view.

How It Works

Mr. Fred, a second grade teacher, taught his children that making a sacrifice meant they would choose between two important things. About a week after the concept was taught, one child stayed in from recess to tell the teacher about a sacrifice he was making.

"There are four of us in the neighborhood, and we decided when we shoveled snow for the neighbors that we would save the money and give it to someone who needs it. We have $17 in our box now and I just wanted you to know that." Mr. Fred complimented the boy and said, "You must feel very proud of the sacrifice you are making. Is this skill difficult for you to do?"

"Heck, no," said the boy. "In fact, I'm making a sacrifice right now."

"You are?" asked the teacher.

"Yes, he replied. "My class is out at recess and I'm in here telling you about the sacrifice I made."

The Motives of Maimonides

Share with students the eight motives that Maimonides, a Jewish philosopher, noticed as he observed people who did acts of kindness. Not everyone gives with the same spirit of selflessness.

1. The highest form of charity is to help the poor become self-supporting by lending them money, taking them into partnership, or giving them work, for in this way there is no loss of self-respect.

2. We should give in such a way that neither the giver nor the one who receives knows the identity of the other.

3. We should give in such a way that the one who received does not know who has given to him or her.

4. We should give in such a way that the giver does not know to whom he or she is giving.

5. We should give before being asked to.

6. Give only after being asked to.

7. Give less than is fitting, but give willingly.

8. Give but give grudgingly.

Activities

Check Student Awareness

Talk with students about the value of sacrificing. Ask:

- What does it mean to sacrifice?
- When you hear the words sacrifice, serve others, volunteer, do these words mean something positive or negative to you? Explain your answer.
- Have you seen anyone in your family or neighborhood make a sacrifice this past week? What did they do? What did they give up? What did they gain?
- Describe a time when you made a sacrifice.

Share Personal Sacrifices

Tell the children why you wanted to be a catechist or teacher. Let them know what you gave up to do this task. More importantly, let them know what you gained because you made this choice.

At home, tell each of your children what it was like on the day they were born. Recreate both the feelings and the facts of the situation. Describe concerns, anxieties, joys, and feelings. Let your children know what you gave up to become a parent and what you gained.

Create a Picture and Article Collage

Place a pile of old magazines and newspapers in the center of the table. Also put out a wide assortment of colored pencils, scissors, glue, and a large sheet of construction paper.

Define the word sacrifice as an act of giving something up in order to gain something equally as good or better. Challenge your family or class to cut out stories and photos of people today who are making sacrifices so life will be better for the coming generations. Discuss:

- What does the word "sacrifice" mean?
- What are two reasons why sacrifice is an important life skill for people to develop?
- What are some other examples of people who are making sacrifices today so that others may live better tomorrow?

- An activity the class as a whole, or students and their families, can do for others.

Volunteering

One of the best ways to show the skill of making sacrifices is to give of your time to help others. This week, make a list of projects or organizations that are in need of volunteer help. Select one that the family or class would be willing to take on as a project for the next few weeks. Invite each person to do a task to learn more about what is needed. Then challenge yourself to make a commitment to help with the project.

When the volunteer time or project has been completed, talk about what you all learned.

Use Children's Literature

Challenge students to find a children's book or story that will illustrate the self-discipline skill of making a sacrifice. Some suggestions are:

A Symphony of Whales, Steve Schuch. This story, based on an actual event, tells of a dramatic rescue, a tale of bravery and faith, and the power of music. When Beluga whales are trapped in a bay, the village people keep the ice open until a Russian ice-breaker can arrive to rescue them.

Buffalo Woman, Paul Goble. This story is part of Native American folklore, a telling tale of the relationship between the buffalo and the Native American people.

Mother Teresa: Helping the Poor, William Jacobs. A biography of the woman who dedicated her life to helping others in India and around the world. Photographs show conditions in which she worked. Several books about Mother Teresa are available for all reading levels.

The Giving Tree, Shel Silverstein. Silverstein has written a timeless parable about the art of giving and not asking for anything in return. The tree sacrifices itself freely and lovingly to a young boy, until the tree has nothing left to give.

Use Music

Teach children this song about service created by Jo Mersnick, sung to the tune of "Baa! Baa! Black Sheep!"

Service to Others

SER - VICE TO OTH-ERS What can I do? Give of my time and spend it with you. SER - VICE TO OTH - ERS What can it be? Give some-thing spe-cial to you from me. SER - VICE TO OTH - ERS What can I say? Ask the ques-tion "How can I help you to - day?"